The Politics of the Urban Crisis

Andrew Sills
Gillian Taylor
Peter Golding

Hutchinson

London   Melbourne   Auckland   Johannesburg

Hutchinson Education

An imprint of Century Hutchinson Ltd

62–65 Chandos Place, London WC2N 4NW

Century Hutchinson Australia Pty Ltd
PO Box 496, 16–22 Church Street, Hawthorn,
Victoria 3122, Australia

Century Hutchinson New Zealand Ltd
PO Box 40–086, Glenfield, Auckland 10,
New Zealand

Century Hutchinson South Africa (Pty) Ltd
PO Box 337, Bergvlei 2012, South Africa

First published 1988
© Andrew Sills, Gillian Taylor and Peter Golding 1988

Set in Linotron Times Roman by
Input Typesetting Ltd, London SW19 8DR

Printed and bound in Great Britain by
Anchor Brendon Ltd, Tiptree, Essex

British Library Cataloguing in Publication Data

Sills, Andrew
    The politics of the urban crisis.
    1. Great Britain. Cities. Inner areas. Social
    planning. Policies of government, 1967–1987
    2. United States. Cities. Inner areas. Social
    planning. Policies of government, 1967–1987
    I. Title   II. Taylor, Gillian   III. Golding,
    Peter
    307′.12
    ISBN 0 09 173129 1

Dedications

To Frank with thanks. A.F.S.

To Kate and Thomas, whose arrival beat the book's.
G.T.

For Ruth, whose turn it is. P.G.

Contents

Acknowledgements   vii

Introduction   ix

Part One   1

1   The urban question: old problems and new
    solutions   3

2   Urban politics goes critical   21

3   The IAP: fiscal crisis and symbolic reassurance   38

Part Two   65

4   A programme without a policy   67

5   Local economic policies: reversing the 'engines
    of exodus'?   91

6   The public and the programme   130

7   Conclusions   165

Bibliography   172

Index   179

Acknowledgements

This book could not have been produced without the active help and support of many people too numerous to mention individually by name. Some special assistance must be singled out for public acknowledgement however.

The research on which the book draws formed a five-year programme of work at the Centre for Mass Communication Research, Leicester University. It was funded by Leicester City Council, who never ceased to support the work, however unflattering some of its findings proved to be. The temptation to shoot the messenger must have been great at times, and it is much to the Council's credit that alone of the authorities administering an Inner Area Programme, it had the courage and foresight to support a fully independent and comprehensive research project to examine the process and impact of the Programme in its area. We owe a particular debt to the Reverend Kenneth Middleton and to Peter Soulsby, respectively leader and deputy leader of the Council at the outset of the research. Many council officers made significant contributions to our work, not always intentionally perhaps, but mostly with great courtesy and tolerance. Hugh Polehampton and Philip Champness, successive leaders of the city's Inner Area Team, merit our special gratitude for stimulating and helpful support.

To our colleagues at the Centre we owe a particular debt for their understanding and charity towards what must at times have seemed something of a cuckoo in the research nest. That what hatched was something more handsome is in no small measure due to the work of Maryrose Tarpey, who worked as Research Associate on the project in its earlier stages and whose technical expertise and personal skills sustained the work and her colleagues through some difficult times initially. Maryrose is in many ways a fourth author of this book and we owe her a great deal.

Acknowledgements

So many people in Leicester helped and gave of their time to assist the research that it would require something the length of an Inner Area Programme Submission Document to list them all. Suffice to say we would wish to acknowledge the help of the many individuals and projects who gave us information and co-operation in the course of the research.

We would like to thank Liz Madder for her efficient and speedy production of the typescript, never easy when collating the work of a dispersed team of authors. We would also like to acknowledge the patient and consistent support of Claire L'Enfant, our editor at Hutchinson, who never wavered in her expectation of delivery, no matter how uncertain the gestation. Needless to say, none of the above is more than indirectly responsible for what follows which represents the views and analysis of the authors alone.

Andrew Sills
Gillian Taylor
Peter Golding
October 1987

Introduction

Barely was the count completed in the 1987 election than the victoriously returned Prime Minister was sounding the central theme of her new administration. 'Something must be done', declared Mrs Thatcher on the steps of Conservative central office in the small hours of the morning after the election, 'about the inner city.' The urban problem was back on top of the political agenda.

In the weeks following the election, despite the relative invisibility of the issue during the campaign, policy for the inner cities became a major priority. Characteristically, Mrs Thatcher herself took the chair of the Cabinet Committee set up to co-ordinate the work of the seven ministries carving up the inner city action between them. For the more cynical observer, there was an underlying electoral imperative behind this flurry of activity. Despite the relative landslide proportions of the Conservative victory, the party found itself after the election without a single seat in Manchester, Liverpool, Glasgow, Newcastle, Bradford and Leicester, only one in Sheffield, and two in each of Leeds and Edinburgh. Within days the party chairman, Norman Tebbitt, launched a recruiting drive in the inner cities aimed at the 'lack of political balance' in these areas.

But such actions and concerns were hardly new. In January 1986, the Prime Minister was chairing a special Cabinet Committee on inner city problems following much deliberation after the recent riots in Handsworth and Tottenham. This in turn was only the latest of many such high profile committees. As the *Economist* had wryly remarked a few weeks earlier about this latest venture, 'Whenever the Prime Minister has a problem she wishes would go away she tells Lord Whitelaw to chair a committee on it' (23 November 1985).

The 1980s had been splattered by a deluge of quangos and

committees launching new attacks on Britain's urban problem. The picture of severe decline was real enough. Between 1951 and 1981 urban areas lost 2 million manufacturing jobs, half of them from inner city areas. Inner city unemployment had risen to 50 per cent above a national average itself leaping upward, and by 1981 nearly 40 per cent of the jobs that remained in the inner cities were performed by commuters. Disinvestment, unemployment, physical decay and social and economic deprivation of chronic proportions were endemic in inner city areas.

Nobody was left out in their expression of concern about the inner cities. The Church of England spoke out forcefully in its controversial report *Faith in the City* (1985), and the Prince of Wales, enlarging on his role as president of Business in the Community and the Prince's Trust, was conducting highly publicized walkabouts culminating in his call, in 1987, for nothing less than 'an urgent crusade' to regenerate the inner cities.

The repeated failure of earlier initiatives was often the starting point for architects of new policies. Peter Walker, who had initiated the Inner Area studies when in the Heath government, in 1972, wrote four years later, to the Labour Prime Minister, James Callaghan, to voice his despair that despite all the various special area-based schemes to help the cities 'unemployment has increased, the housing conditions have got worse, the crime rate has soared to new heights, and we are making no substantial breakthrough as far as education is concerned' (Higgins *et al.* 1983, p. 121).

In 1977 a decade of hectic activity was launched by the then Secretary of State for the Environment, Peter Shore. In a number of important speeches in 1976 and 1977, Shore had expounded on the urban problem in visionary terms. 'If cities fail', he argued, 'so to a large extent does our society' (DoE press release no. 835). He warned a conference in February 1977 that 'the consequences of turning our back on the inner areas would, in my judgement, be likely to be mounting social bitterness, an increasing sense of alienation, worsening crime and vandalism, and, in some areas, racial tension as well' (quoted in Higgins *et al.* 1983, p. 126). Shore's White Paper, *Policy for the Inner Cities* (Cmnd 6845) was published in June 1977. It proposed to 'give a new priority in the main policies and programmes of government so that they contribute to a better life in the inner areas'. The resulting scheme of Inner Area programmes and Partnerships is the subject of this book.

Our scope is a modest one. We do not aim to address the many fruitful and extensive debates which have flourished in recent years as a result of the renaissance of urban theory. There are many excellent accounts, both primary and secondary, of these debates (e.g. Dunleavy 1980; Saunders 1981). Equally, we do not aim at as broad a target as the many valuable accounts chronicling the twists and turns of urban policy since the war (e.g. Edwards and Batley 1978; Lawless 1981; Rees and Lambert 1985). Our concern is with one particular, if peculiarly significant, initiative, the Inner Area Programme (IAP).

The book is presented in two parts. In Part One, we examine the genealogy and political background to the IAP. Chapters 1 and 2 examine the ideas and practices bequeathed to recent urban policy from forerunners in the United States and from predecessors to the IAP, and demonstrate the shift in rhetoric and reality as the new programmes were formed. Chapter 3 turns to the political economy of the IAP, and suggests it has been determined as much by the fiscal and ideological priorities of the state as by the needs of inner city areas.

Part Two provides a detailed case study of the operation of the IAP in one city, Leicester. Based on a five-year research programme we analyse the political, social and economic dimensions of the programme in close focus to display not merely the anatomy but the entrails of urban policy in actual practice. Chapter 4 deals with the political mechanics of the programme and the relationship between the local authority implementing the programme and the government departments and local agencies with which it has to deal. Chapter 5 examines public involvement in the programme, and explores the reality of community and voluntary sector partnership with statutory agencies. Chapter 6 addresses the question of to what extent the IAP can achieve the economic regeneration of the inner areas which is at the heart of its intentions, and discusses the dilemmas created in attempts to implement innovative local economic initiatives.

The study begins with an account of the relationship between poverty programmes and urban policy.

Part One

1 The urban question: old problems and new solutions

The winter of 1885/6 was the coldest for thirty years. The docks and building industry in London were virtually idle and the depression was at its most severe. A meeting of the unemployed in Trafalgar Square on 8 February called for public works and tariff barriers and marched to Hyde Park to disperse. Very quickly the meeting turned into a riot. The smart club windows in Pall Mall and St James's were stoned, carriages were overturned and shops looted as the rioters wound their destructive and angry way back towards the East End. Over the next two days respectable London withdrew behind boarded-up shop windows as the troops were made ready and magistrates dusted off the riot act. The 'dangerous classes' had sounded a warning. The urban problem was visibly stalking the streets of the capital (Golding and Middleton 1982, pp. 19–31; Stedman Jones 1976, pp. 291 ff.).

By the middle of the nineteenth century there were more people living in towns than in the country. The concentrations of people in urban areas produced whole new ways of living and experience that were to change every dimension of political and social life. The cities were forever to be a problem. The threat of the mob was central to this problem, prompting Chamberlain's famous rhetorical question in Birmingham in 1885, 'What ransom will property pay for the security which it enjoys?' (Gulley 1926, pp. 213–14). At the root were the residuum 'recruited from the incapable or immoral who have fallen out of the ranks of respectable labour' as *The Times* described them (6 February 1886).

What was needed was something to 'take the steam out of sedition' as George Bernard Shaw put it (*Pall Mall Gazette*, 11 February 1886), since, as the paper remarked the following day, 'To sit on the safety valve is not the best means of preventing an explosion.' But the urban poor were not merely a problem, they were also an expression of the hopelessness and inhumanity of

3

the new urban life. It was this new barbarism that had so dismayed Engels in London and Manchester.

Everywhere barbarous indifference, hard egotism on one hand, and nameless misery on the other, everywhere social warfare, every man's house in a state of siege, everywhere reciprocal plundering under the protection of the law, and all so shameless, so openly avowed that one shrinks before the consequences of our social state as they manifest themselves here undisguised, and can only wonder that the whole crazy fabric still hangs together. (Engels 1969, p. 58)

This was Gissing's 'great gloomy city', which, for its hapless inhabitants, Wells concluded, 'showed no gleam of hope of anything . . . but dinginess until they died' (see Williams 1975, ch. 19). The city remained a conundrum. On the one hand it was a place of opportunity, paved with gold, a magnet for the enterprising, ambitious and diligent. On the other it was a place of despair, a melting pot of all that was wretched and dismal in the human condition. And always it was a place of fear; fear of the dangerous classes whose threatening potential Samuel Smith foresaw so clearly. 'The time may come when the neglect of these social issues will exact a terrible revenge on the wealthier classes. . . . If we do not drain away the foul sewage that stagnates at the base of our social fabric, we inevitably prepare terrible disasters for our descendants' (Smith 1883, pp. 911–12).

Our concern here is with how Chamberlain's ransom was paid in the urban policy of a century after these fears were first so graphically expressed. We cannot here trace the many shifts and turns of policy through the years in between. However, we do need to begin with an account of the immediate forebears of recent British urban policy, in its various attempts to cope with urban threat and despair.

'The paradox of poverty in the midst of plenty': learning from the other America

Post-war reconstruction stimulated economic growth and brought a new confidence to the international economy. The belief in progress that had been lost in the depression of the thirties returned once more, bolstered by a faith in the ability of governments to apply the lessons of war-time planning to winning the peace. Armed now with Keynesian economics, demand would not be allowed to oscillate, it would be 'fine tuned'. Yet, although there was a rapid rise in real wages throughout the western world, the 1950s was a decade of increasing insecurity. Whilst political tensions focused initially on the external threat posed by the Bomb and the Cold War, there was a growing unease about a threat from within. Despite economic growth there remained a persistent poverty that refused to be shifted. Concentrated in the inner city this poverty was made the more visible by its colour. In America there had been a mass migration of blacks to the Northern cities, whilst in Britain there was an increasing level of immigration from the Empire. In both the combined operation of the economic and housing markets ensured the concentration of these migrants in certain sections of the cities, which in turn evoked fears of an alien presence from the white middle classes who moved increasingly to the suburbs. The concern for law and order in the cities, seen within a specific racial context, found expression in Britain in the Notting Hill Riots in 1958. However, it was in the United States in the 1960s where the collapse of civil order was most dramatic. As the ghettos burned through the summer nights and thousands of national guard troopers enforced the curfew, the 'urban crisis' had reappeared.

This chapter is concerned with examining a particular form of state response to the 'urban crisis', the poverty programme, through which central government provides limited resources to fund special projects in the ghettos with the aim of postponing or deflecting the likelihood of street violence. This method of tackling the 'urban crisis', through programmes of selective urban aid, was first introduced in the United States in the 1960s. The American experience warrants examination for three reasons; firstly, the American poverty programme rehearses many of the issues and arguments that have been central to the British experience. Many of the problems encountered with Urban Aid, Community Development Projects (CDP) and the Inner Area Programme (IAP) surfaced for the first time in the United States. Secondly, whilst the British acknowledge the influence of the American model, they appear to have learnt little from the experiment, duplicating many of the same mistakes. Examining the experiences of poverty programmes in both countries highlights the advantages administrators and politicians saw in this type of action, and also the problems they both share. Finally, with the

American initiative being larger, more ambitious and less constrained, its political objectives and motivations are more visible than in its British counterpart.

Whilst the post-war years had brought a rising standard of living for many Americans, the benefits of economic growth had not been evenly distributed, either by race or by area. Official estimates of the number in poverty in 1960 was 39 million, or 21 per cent of the population (Paterson 1981, p. 20). Whilst poverty was growing in real terms, it was at the same time becoming concentrated amongst the black populations in the ghettos of the Northern cities. The modernization of Southern agriculture had witnessed a massive decline in the demand for labour that prompted the mass emigration to the North. Between 1940 and 1965 the blacks 'became an urban people' as 20 million left the land in search of work. Their arrival in the North coincided with the introduction of automation in many industrial processes and the slackening of demand for unskilled labour. This had an adverse and cumulative affect on the economic position of the blacks.

Whilst in 1940 black unemployment was 20 per cent higher than amongst whites, this had risen to 71 per cent by 1953. By 1963, it was twice as high, when Moynihan observed that a two to one unemployment ratio between blacks and whites was now 'frozen into the economy' (Marris and Rein 1967, p. 34). At the same time, the median income for the black population was only half that of the whites. The spatial concentration of poverty amongst the black population was accentuated by two factors. Firstly, there was the flight to the suburbs of the affluent middle class and the unionized and skilled working class. Secondly, there were the various urban renewal or 'negro removal' schemes which attempted to redevelop the central business districts and modernize the city's infrastructure, entailing the demolition of many of the tenement blocks to make way for offices and motorways. As in nineteenth-century London, slum clearance resulted in a worsening of housing standards for the poor who could neither afford the higher rents or transport costs associated with suburban housing and were forced to find accommodation from a decreasing supply in the inner city.

The existence of poverty was given widespread publicity by Michael Harrington in his book *The Other America* (1962). In it he claimed that there was a substantial degree of poverty in

America, but that this went unnoticed because the poor were invisible and silent. He argued that whilst economic growth had eradicated the mass poverty of the 1930s, there existed a 'new' poor, made up of groups like the elderly, single parent families and minority groups who lived in the 'other America', the ghetto.

There had been comparatively little concern for the poor during the 1950s, many of whom encountered strong resistance to their registration on the welfare rolls. It would appear that poverty by itself was of insufficient political priority to warrant additional resources. Whilst there was concern for the increased concentration of poverty in the black ghettos, it took street violence and the breakdown of law and order to provoke a response. In the late 1950s this concern for public order in the ghetto centred on the problems of juvenile delinquency and the urban gang, which acted as a focus for middle-class fears about youth, blacks and violence in the city. It prompted a series of special project programmes which were forerunners to the fuller poverty programmes of the 1960s.

West Side Story?

As the economic conditions in the ghettos deteriorated this had the effect of undermining traditional family structures. Thus, the proportion of black female-headed families increased, particularly in the cities. 'In 1960, 23.1 per cent of urban black families was headed by females, compared with 11.1 per cent in rural farm areas' (Piven and Cloward 1972, p. 225). Among the poorest families in the larger cities this figure rose to well over half.

A series of interrelated problems was seen to result from the weakening of the family's function of social control: 'rising rates of gang delinquency and other forms of juvenile delinquency, such as school vandalism; spreading drug addiction; an alarming increase in serious crimes, such as armed robbery and burglary' (Piven and Cloward 1972, p. 226). Moynihan describes how fear of black violence was 'to become a near obsession of white America', and this found expression in juvenile delinquency and the fighting gang (Moynihan 1969, p. 14). His explanation for this depth of concern was that juvenile delinquency became a symbol that unified many of the social and moral dangers of the decade. Just as America was facing an external threat from communism, she was being weakened from within by a disintegration in community and traditional values.

Urban life was producing the symptoms of alienation and anomie that were destroying the old mediating structures, such as family and community, that integrated individuals into society. At the same time, there were developing new alien communities, with their own codes of behaviour, dress and shared values that presented both a moral and physical challenge to the American way of life. This could be celebrated, as in *West Side Story*, but was more usually condemned.

Concern for the problems of juvenile delinquency had an important influence on the development of the poverty programmes. Through delinquency were reflected the same fears of urban violence that reappeared with riots in the following decade. Research into the problems of delinquency that stressed the importance of societal causes had a liberalizing impact on attitudes to a whole range of social problems and pointed to the need for more government action, which came in the form of special project programmes.

The pathological view of the delinquent as the deviant outside of society was subsequently challenged: 'Delinquency could be interpreted either as an illegitimate attempt to secure the symbols of prestige, or as a retreat from the struggle. Thus the causes of delinquency were taken out of the context of individual pathology and reinterpreted in terms of inequality in economic and educational opportunity' (quoted in Marris and Rein 1967, pp. 43–4).

This was an attempt to reclaim the delinquent back into society. In essence, the delinquents had the 'right' motives in their desire to aspire to the American Dream; they merely lacked the ability to compete in the free market and earn their success through legitimate channels. This reinterpretation of delinquency as a social rather than a psychological problem had major implications for how this and other social problems should be tackled, so that there was a case for positive discrimination in public services in favour of deprived groups to compensate for the deficiencies elsewhere in their lives. A two-year programme of action and research, Mobilization for Youth, was launched by the National Institute of Mental Health, and this was to have an influential demonstration effect as a forerunner to the future poverty programmes.

The funding of projects to combat delinquency coincided with a wider initiative to tackle the social problems of the city sponsored by the Ford Foundation. In the 1950s the Public Affairs Department of the Ford Foundation became concerned about the delining state of American cities, focusing on the 'grey areas' or inner city. These grey areas became 'a symbol of hope abandoned, alienation and retreat' (Marris and Rein 1967, p. 38). The Ford Foundation had a long tradition of philanthropy in the United States and now proposed to use its resources to revive the cities. There were two central concepts that guided the Ford Foundation in their attempts to find an answer to the problems of these 'grey areas'. Firstly, it was argued that the residents of the 'grey areas' lived in the grip of the poverty cycle from which it was hard to escape. Those who were born into poverty were at such a disadvantage that they were likely to remain in poverty throughout their lives. Secondly, it was presumed that government services were inflexible and inefficient and could not alone break the cycle of poverty.

Given both the size of the task and their limited resources, the Ford Foundation based its intervention upon a series of experimental demonstration projects:

The Ford Foundation projects set out to show how the city might redeem its broken promise. They sought to challenge the conservatism of an impoverished school system; open worthwhile careers to young people disillusioned by neglect; return public and private agencies to a relevant and coherent purpose; and encourage a respect for the rights and dignity of the poor. The projects could not claim, in themselves, to realize so ambitious a programme of reform. But they proposed to demonstrate – in neighbourhoods of five cities and one state – how the problems might be solved. (Marris and Rein 1967, p. 38)

Here we can see for the first time the formula used by the poverty programmes on both sides of the Atlantic.

The problems of the inner city are tackled through special projects designed to break into the cycle of poverty at key points whilst performing action research experiments which will have a demonstration effect for other voluntary and public services. Together, the Ford Foundation's Grey Areas Project and the Mobilization for Youth initiative were extremely influential in suggesting both a new interpretation of social problems and the way these problems might be tackled.

The Great Society: the response to urban crisis

As the 1950s drew to a close there was increasing concern about
a number of issues that seemed, in the minds of middle-class
Americans, to converge in both a racial context and an urban
location. The paradox of 'poverty in the midst of plenty', the
perceived collapse of community values and the breakdown of
family structures, the threat to public order and the spectre of
racial unrest all focused attention on the blacks in the ghetto. As
these problems increased, the private response was the flight to
the suburbs leaving the inner city as 'the sink' for those with
nowhere else to go.

In 1960, John F. Kennedy was elected President by the
narrowest of majorities, in a victory which owed much to the
black vote. Whilst the democrats had continued to lose support
in the rural and suburban areas they gained in the large cities,
particularly from the black vote. However, during his first two
years in office Kennedy did very little on either civil rights or
welfare issues. This was to change dramatically with the outbreak
of violence in the cities, which posed a particular problem for the
Democratic Party. If they were to stay in office it was crucial that
they consolidate their urban power base. However, if the cities
were the Democrats' strength, they were also their weakness
because it was in the cities that the government was facing a
severe credibility test.

The solution for this legitimation crisis was sought in a series
of poverty programmes which directed federal aid towards the
disaffected in the big city ghettos. This was, in essence, a political
response to a political problem, that of 'urban crisis'. Whilst there
are many factors that contribute to an outbreak of rioting, a riot
is, above all else, a political act which symbolizes the collapse of
consent and the rejection of established channels for addressing
grievances. From the state's viewpoint, riots pose major problems.
Although law and order can be restored in the short term by force,
the day-to-day operation of a country's economic and political
processes relies on consent rather than coercion. The problem
was how to win back the consent of the disaffected in the ghettos.
This required a political response which was made through the
poverty programmes. The government tried, through the use of
federal funds, to draw dissent off the streets and back into the
legitimate political arena, and, if possible, into the Democratic

fold. The political objective of directed patronage has been of primary importance to the poverty programmes on both sides of the Atlantic, but found its clearest statement in the Great Society programmes in America. These will be examined below in the context of the state's response to urban crisis.

Between 1964 and 1968 violence in American cities was commonplace, 239 riots took place which were serious enough for the local police to seek outside assistance. 'The burning, looting and small area fires that blitzed her cities in the mid-1960s reached levels of domestic violence which were virtually unprecedented' (Sears and McConahy 1973, p. 182). One of the most serious of these was in the Watts district of Los Angeles in 1965. The riot started after the police had been heavy-handed in making an arrest. A crowd gathered, a scene developed and batons were used. As reinforcements were called in the crowd stoned the police and the riot was under way. During the six days that followed, 34 people were killed, 1032 people were seriously injured and there was an estimated $40 million damage to property. It took 13,900 national guardsmen, 934 police and 719 sheriff's deputies to contain the riot by imposing a curfew over a district covering 46.5 square miles (Sears and McConahy, 1973, p. 9).

Whilst the social and economic conditions in the ghettos were major contributory factors to the riots, the principal cause and impact was political. This is demonstrated by two factors. Firstly, poverty does not always provoke violence. There had been, for example, a lack of disorder in the South where the comparatively slow decline in the demand for labour had brought no need for sudden adjustment. The dispersed nature of the rural population made control easy for the quasi-feudal regime, who could back up legal power with physical coercion. However, 'Only when the unemployed rural workers had migrated to the central cities where they concentrated in the ghettos, did turmoil erupt' (Piven and Cloward 1971, p. 212). The political impact of the riots was enormous. The Watts riots covered a large area and involved many thousands of people either actively or as sympathetic bystanders. Thus, a large section of the city witnessed, at first hand, the collapse of consent. This experience, duplicated again and again in other cities, provided a clear threat to the legitimacy of government.

Secondly, research which followed in the aftermath of the riots revealed that for the participants the riots represented a political statement, a rejection of a biased political system. Sears and McConahy (1973) found amongst the active participants in the Watts riot a 'generalised political disaffection' (p. 205) that was concerned with societal rather than personal problems. The rioters came, principally, from the ranks of the 'New Urban Blacks' and not from the very poorest classes, and tended to have had an above average level of education. They displayed a political sophistication and a positive attitude towards their black identity which contrasted with the more fatalistic views of their older counterparts. They had lost faith in the political system in which the rules operated against them and in an economic system which denied them equal opportunities because of their colour. For them the riots were an act of political rejection.

By this time Lyndon Johnson was President and commanded a huge majority. His problem was how to handle this collapse of consent without alienating his urban electorate:

Many of these riots occurred in or near urban renewal areas, and they constituted a kind of revolt against the heritage of the New Deal urban programs. They certainly showed that Johnson's most critically located and supportive political constituency could be extremely volatile. Such events led Johnson to make choices that his predecessors, Truman and Roosevelt, would not or could not make. (Mollenkopf 1983, p. 84)

Johnson chose to revive the Democrat tradition of using federal finance both to tackle urban problems and build up new electoral alliances, prompting the Republican taunt of 'spend, spend, spend, elect, elect, elect'.

Urban politics in the United States was built around the party machine, which could both influence and organize the new immigrant vote in the expanding Northern cities. However, as the machine ran on patronage it presented a major constraint to attempts to broaden the appeal of a party beyond the influence of its machine. In the thirties, Roosevelt recognized that if the Democratic Party was to capture all the important urban votes, it needed a way of delivering its patronage to a broader audience over the heads of its own political machine. The answer was found in federal urban development policy, which could be used to buy urban votes under the laudable pretext of responding to the problems of the Depression:

Federal urban development programmes have provided a principal method – perhaps the key method – by which national Democratic political entrepreneurs have attempted to widen and organize their political support. Urban programs enabled Democrats to build national political power on a base of urban electoral majorities, and to sustain that influence over time through new non-party organizational forms. (Mollenkopf 1983, p. 48)

Thus, from its earliest days, a mixture of motives have prompted governments to support urban development programmes. As one of Roosevelt's advisers remarked: 'We were confronted with a choice between an orderly revolution – a peaceful and rapid departure from the past concepts – and a violent and disorderly overthrow of the whole capitalist structure' (Mollenkop 1983, p. 158).

The same combination of factors – growing poverty, the fear of urban disorder and racial unrest, together with the need to secure new electoral alliances – prompted the Democratic Party to introduce its poverty programme in the 1960s. The major difference now was that the problem was more explicitly political and required a rapid and local response. To bypass the alleged bias in local political systems, the federal government chose to employ the mechanism of a special projects programme to ensure that patronage was delivered to the correct political target.

The federal response came through a series of special programmes, all aimed at directing resources to the problems and voters in the inner city. Each was launched as a White House initiative, the President using his powers to design new programmes which were then given massive publicity to justify the action. The earliest of these programmes was introduced in 1961 when the problems of juvenile delinquency were to be tackled by youth development projects in the inner city, followed in 1963 by programmes that addressed the issue of mental health by setting up community health centres, again in the inner city. The policy gathered momentum under President Johnson with the Economic Opportunity Act 1964, the anti-poverty programme. This was to 'eliminate the paradox of poverty in the midst of plenty in this Nation by opening to everyone the opportunity for education and training, the opportunity to work, and the opportunity to live in decency and dignity.'

The Act launched a whole host of government schemes of which the most significant was the Community Action Programme

(CAP). With the incentive of 90 per cent federal funding, new projects were to be created in the inner city that would involve government and voluntary agencies and, most crucially, the poor themselves. The call for the 'maximum feasible participation' of residents in the designing and running of projects was to be the most controversial aspect of the entire poverty programme. When residents did start to challenge professional decisions and political structures, predictably 'all hell broke loose'. Political bosses, like Major Daley of Chicago, who had campaigned hard to get the anti-poverty funds, now found that the very projects he had helped to set up were challenging his power. Thus, to an extent, the CAP had succeeded in its principal aim of reaching over the heads of local as well as state government, directing resources to the neighbourhood level.

In 1966, the Model Cities programme was introduced which called for a 'Comprehensive attack on social, economic and physical problems in selected slums and blighted areas through the most effective and economical concentration and coordination of Federal, State, local and private efforts . . . to develop model neighbourhoods in the deteriorated cores of the central cities' (Piven and Cloward 1967, p. 257). This attempted to avoid some of the conflicts caused by participation by channelling funds to the ghetto through local government. In both its method and motives it can be seen as the direct ancestor to the IAP. Finally, in 1967 President Johnson launched the Neighborhood Service Program, which was to provide for a co-ordinated attack on the problem of the slums.

Behind these apparently separate presidential initiatives there were striking similarities both in the way in which they were organized and in the direction of their resources. Firstly, although they claimed to be tackling the problems associated with poverty, the resources went, almost without exception, to the urban ghettos. Whilst there was no arguing with the substantial degree of deprivation in these large urban centres, the exclusion of rural areas where poverty was equally extreme was significant. Why were the urban poor to have a special priority? Secondly, why was it necessary to create separate programmes to tackle these 'urban problems' when there already existed a whole range of government agencies with expertize and funds that were meant to be addressing the problems? If they were failing because of lack of funds they should have priority for additional resources rather than establishing new programmes. Alternatively, if existing programmes were proving ineffective, then the solution should be to change rather than bypass them.

The explanation for both the urban bias and the style of funding of poverty programmes was a political one. The primary purpose of these programmes was not to tackle poverty but to respond directly, at comparatively low cost, to the crisis of consent posed by the riots.

We have seen that the size of the black migration and its concentration in the Northern ghettos made the mass of black poor a political force to be reckoned with, both through the ballot box and on the streets. In its attempts to defuse urban violence and secure new alliances with the black community, the Democratic Party developed a series of programmes that sought to reach the ghetto voters over the heads of the city governments and their political machines. As a political problem the 'urban crisis' required a political solution, which was to involve the poor directly in these programmes as a means of redistributing power and patronage in the city.

The British experience

Observers in England have for many years treated events across the Atlantic as a form of cultural weather-vane that could point in the direction of future change. The outbreak of urban violence in a specifically racial context was of obvious concern in Britain in the 1960s, when the issue of immigration from the Commonwealth was forcing itself onto the political agenda. The connection between fears of racial violence and poverty programmes was forged when, three weeks after Enoch Powell delivered his 'Rivers of Blood' speech, Harold Wilson announced the first of the government's new initiatives, Urban Aid. Since 1968 there has been a whole series of small-scale experimental programmes that have sought to tackle 'urban' problems on an area basis, the IAP (1977) being the largest and most ambitious.

These programmes share many similarities with their American counterparts both in their style (low cost, high profile programmes, funded jointly by central and local government), and their motivation (a desire to prevent racial violence under the disguise of concern for urban deprivation). Indeed, the parallels are so striking that it is questionable why so little appears to have been learnt in each country by the mistakes made in the other. The major difference, however, between the poverty programmes in the two countries concerns their relationship with the main programme activities of public agencies. We have seen how in the United States poverty programmes were used by the federal government as a means of directing its resources into the ghettos without the interference of state government. The situation in Britain differs in two crucial respects: firstly, the power of central government is much stronger relative to local authorities, so that it can intervene more directly at the local level than the federal government in the United States and, secondly, there has been in Britain a far greater commitment to the role and contribution of public services.

Because of the concern about the apparent inability of existing programmes to tackle the problems of deprivation, as such, one of the main tasks of the poverty programmes in Britain was to experiment, in order to inform and redirect the main programme activities of government. Whilst in America the main thrust for the poverty programmes came from the politicians, in Britain the contribution of the professional administrator is of far greater importance.

Reassessing the Welfare State

Whilst the country was allegedly 'Never having it so good', research evidence was questioning the assumption that the post-war boom had eradicated poverty. Just as in the United States, greater affluence had not brought greater equality. The work of Townsend and Abel Smith demonstrated that the number of people with incomes below national assistance rates had trebled between 1953–54 and 1960. Yet the 'rediscovery of poverty' did not lead to a demand for improved benefits, but rather a call for greater selectivity. The Welfare State had been constructed around a national system of social insurance, based on universal rather than means tested benefits. This system was expensive and it was felt to have failed to eradicate poverty. Rather than endure the massive costs of an increase in benefits to all, it was argued that a more selective approach was required, improving the conditions of the very poor.

Whilst the rediscovery of poverty was primarily about income maintenance, the depressing reassessment of post-war achievements was reinforced by a series of reports on various aspects of the Welfare State, such as in housing (Milner Holland Report, *Housing in Greater London*, 1958), education (Plowden Report, *Children and Their Primary Schools*, 1966) and social services (Seebohm Report, *Local Authority and Allied Personal Services*, 1968). In each case the reports concluded that state services were failing to reach those in greatest need who were seen to live in small pockets of deprivation in the older cities. If state services were to be instrumental in breaking through the cycle of poverty that gripped these people's lives, then there was a need for far greater selectivity. Thus, at the same time that doubts were being raised about the efficiency of the Welfare State in helping those in greatest need, there was a consensus developing around the advantages of positive discrimination on an area basis.

If the initial interest in the area approach stemmed from a professional concern about the persistence of poverty, the political commitment to the experimental poverty programme came from a different source, the growing fear of racial unrest.

'Rivers of Blood' and urban aid

The post-war boom had resulted in a shortage of labour, so the government encouraged emigration from the Empire to the Home Country in an attempt to free this bottleneck. The weak bargaining position of migrant workers in the labour market forced them to take low paid, unskilled jobs and to rely on the cheap accommodation found in the inner city. As in the United States, the poverty of the black community ensured its concentration, whilst their colour highlighted, for the white community, the changes that were taking place.

The race riots in Notting Hill in 1958 underlined the growing tension felt about the level of immigration. Immigration from the West Indies, India and Pakistan rose from 21,600 in 1959 to 136,400 in 1961, when the Conservative Conference first called for some control (Edwards and Batley, 1978, p. 27). When the Labour Party was returned to power in 1964, they lost the safe seat of Smethwick on the immigration issue. With a parliamentary majority of only three they bowed to public pressure and introduced immigration controls. In 1968, Enoch Powell fanned the fears of mass immigration from Kenya, and the Labour government rushed through a further Commonwealth Immigration Act severely curtailing the right of British passport holders to enter the UK.

In April 1968, Powell delivered his 'Rivers of Blood' speech in which he warned that the concentrations of large numbers of coloured people would bring trouble to the cities. The Labour Party clearly needed a response. Having acknowledged, through its immigration legislation, that immigrants were 'a problem', the Party needed to reaffirm their commitment to integration and to good race relations. An American-style special projects programme offered the advantages of a quick response with a high political profile, together with low costs and a strong degree of central control.

When Harold Wilson announced the Urban Programme (UP) in May 1968, it came as a surprise to Whitehall. Whilst the Home Office had been working on a scheme for positive discrimination, they were uncertain as to what the new initiative implied. Had their ideas been accepted or pre-empted?

Edwards and Batley have identified five major assumptions contained within the Prime Minister's speech which have had a major influence in shaping the UP:

1. Immigrants: the programme was designed to tackle both the problems faced by immigrants, such as bad housing, but also the problems caused by immigrants, such as the strain on services.
2. Multiple deprivation: the programme accepted the conclusions of the Plowden and Seebohm Committees that there were areas in which people suffered from a range of disadvantages.
3. Existing services: the problems of multiple deprivation could be tackled by the existing services of central and local government.
4. Existing processes: the current procedures within government agencies were adequate and did not require examination.
5. No extra resources: the programme should not require large scale resources but should be within the budgets of existing services. (Edwards and Batley 1978, pp. 41–42)

The UP shared certain similarities with the American poverty programmes in its central concern for the problem of racial harmony in the inner city. Indeed, Edwards and Batley suggest that the Urban Aid programme would have been even more explicit about the needs of ethnic minorities if there had not been fears of a white backlash against a blatant policy of positive discrimination. Also, in line with the American approach, the British UP was to be low key in resource terms, for the 'urban crisis' was not to be solved by risking a fiscal crisis. The major differences between the two countries concerned the attitude to existing resources. Whilst these were to be circumvented in the United States, a more cautious approach was adopted in Britain. Existing services and processes were expected to learn from the UP's experiments, but were not, in themselves, under threat or discussion.

The Prime Minister's statement had been one of intent rather than an outline of a new policy, and it was left to a civil service working party to sort out the details. This was chaired by the Home Office, significantly the department with responsibility for immigration and public order. The working party encountered many difficulties. Areas of multiple deprivation appeared elusive. 'One third of the United Kingdom's population was implicated in the first definition of deprived areas!' (Edwards and Batley 1978, p. 50). This hardly accorded with the notion of targeting resources, nor with the level of resources available. Similarly, the list of possible projects for funding through the UP was long, all-embracing and lacked any clear direction.

It was difficult to see how the projects chosen formed a specific programme, as they lacked any focus other than a general concern for either education or ethnic minority issues. The issue of funding was also problematic – whether to give local authorities an enhanced rate support grant allowing them to make the allocation decisions, or to opt for a specific grant system with a greater degree of control from the centre. In the event, the specific grant system was chosen, local authorities, and through them voluntary organizations, submitting projects annually for approval, in accordance with advice received in the annual urban programme circular. This was, in embryo, the model for the IAP a decade later.

In parallel with developments taking place on the UP, a separate Whitehall working party was exploring another approach to poverty. Taking its ideas from the American Poverty

Programme, it was looking at the scope for tackling multiple deprivation on an area basis through community development. The Community Development Project (CDP), as it became known, began in the early 1970s with grand ambitions.

This will be a neighbourhood-based experiment aimed at finding new ways of meeting the needs of people living in areas of high social deprivation; by bringing together the work of all the social services under the leadership of a special project team and also by tapping resources of self help and mutual help which may exist among the people in the neighbourhood. (Home Office 1969)

Local people, with professional assistance, were to be led and motivated to improve their lives via self-help. The teams of academics monitoring these action research projects would ensure that the lessons and achievements of the experiments would be understood and made applicable elsewhere.

In practice, the CDP became a huge embarrassment for government, putting forward analyses of urban deprivation whose implications were politically unacceptable. The spectacular rise of the CDP and its equally spectacular fall (it was unceremoniously closed down by the 1974–9 Labour government) is examined in more detail in Chapter 2. But the fate of the CDP highlights a longer-term phenomenum of successive inner city policies on both sides of the Atlantic – the increasing frustration and dilution of grand ambition and high ideals.

The poverty programmes examined in this chapter were all underwritten originally not only with good intentions but also with a belief that certain new initiatives would actually tackle or eradicate urban deprivation. As new initiatives were generated with increasing frequency, it became clear that the 'problem' to be tackled was both larger and more intractable than first thought, and the 'solutions' put forward more piecemeal and inadequate in comparison. The dilution of grand ideals into pragmatic, cheap and visible urban programmes became a feature of urban social policy in this period. However, as we shall see in the following chapter, this diminution of ambition was to become a much more central factor in the late 1970s and the 1980s.

2 Urban politics goes critical

Introduction

In this chapter we trace the development of urban policy in the UK from the Community Development Project (CDP) in the mid-1970s through to the recent initiatives developed by Prime Minister Thatcher's government in the late 1980s. In particular, we focus on the role and potential of these initiatives as poverty programmes.

From CDP to IAP: redefining urban poverty?

In July 1969 the Home Secretary announced that Coventry, Liverpool and Southwark local authorities would be taking part in neighbourhood-based action-research experiments under the CDP. The aim was to find new ways of meeting the needs of people living in areas of severe deprivation by bringing together the work of all the social services under the leadership of a project team, who worked closely with university research teams, who in turn monitored the project. A central steering group was established which kept in touch with the local teams. Broadly, the CDP was an attempt to combine the effort of national and local government, voluntary organizations and the universities in finding new ways of supplementing or coordinating the existing social services in a neighbourhood. Great emphasis was placed on citizen involvement and self-help. Most of the cost of the projects was met by the urban programme.

At intervals between 1969 and 1972, local CDPs were set up in nine other authorities: Kirklees, Cumbria, Birmingham, North Tyneside, West Glamorgan, Newham, Newcastle upon Tyne, Oldham and Paisley. Whilst the CDPs were developed separately

21

from UA, it was thought useful, for presentational purposes, to link these schemes, and the CDP became in effect the action research element of the Urban Programme (UP). As the initiative for the CDPs came from the civil service rather than from politicians it had a comparatively low level of funding, but the impact of the scheme and the issues it raised were to have far-reaching effects.

The rise and fall of the CDP experiment has been well documented, surrounded as it was by major controversy. At its peak, the project was employing more than 100 action and research staff. By 1978, however, the projects had completed their programmes and were being wound up. The Home Office had become increasingly embarrassed by the radical output from these projects and was clearly glad to see them quietly forgotten (Lawless 1981, ch. 6).

The CDPs' unpopularity with the Home Office was due to reinterpretation by many CDP teams of the Home Office brief, shifting from local 'pump-priming' self-help projects to developing radical programmes. The teams rejected their original brief whose interpretation of deprivation was based on the concept of the pathology of the poor, requiring the building of consensus, the raising of morale, and the promotion of better communication with government to effect an improvement in the life of inner city communities. Instead, several of the teams adopted a radical and sometimes even quasi-Marxist diagnosis which called for community action to redress class inequalities.

The impact of the CDP initiative was far-reaching. The project produced a great wealth of descriptive, analytical and prescriptive material. The most important effect was to promote a new view of deprivation. In place of the social pathology interpretation, the CDP put the blame for deprivation on changes within economic, educational and housing markets, allied to the weak bargaining position of the poor.

Despite its disturbing implications for the government, the work of the CDPs was well researched and hard to ignore. As the economic climate deteriorated and the weaknesses of the British economy were exposed, the movement from a personal to a structural interpretation of deprivation gathered momentum. Thus the CDP accepted that changing employment structures had much to do with urban deprivation: a major departure from previous government views of inner city problems.

The CDPs were thus a watershed in the development of urban

policy in the UK. The three Inner Area Studies commissioned in 1972 by Peter Walker at the DoE provided further empirical evidence which reinforced the more structural view of inner city decay being promulgated by the CDP.

The Inner Area Studies were designed to bring a 'total approach' to urban problems. The studies were organized jointly by the DoE and the local authorities concerned, using outside consultants. The problems of six urban areas were examined. Three of these were complete industrial towns: Oldham, Rotherham and Sunderland. Three were districts of major cities which were known to suffer from multiple deprivation: Small Heath in Birmingham, Lambeth in London and Toxteth in Liverpool. Although much of the Inner Area Studies relate to small-scale projects, the final papers contained a theoretical analysis of the problems in inner cities. The reports were published between 1974 and 1977 (DoE 1977a). The studies underlined the economic decline, physical decay and social problems in parts of Birmingham, Lambeth and Liverpool, and the importance of their findings were acknowledged in the 1977 White Paper on policy for the inner cities.

The Inner Area Studies of urban deprivation were extremely influential in formulating the government's new response to urban deprivation. Being undertaken by professional consultants, these studies were very different from the radical, community-based CDP initiatives. Nevertheless, the final reports of the Inner Area Studies reveal similar analyses to some of the main CDP views on inner area decay. The Inner Area Studies ascribed the root cause of deprivation to basic poverty. Low personal incomes were caused by inadequate social security benefits for disadvantaged groups as well as by rising unemployment due to changes in the local and national labour markets. Thus the Inner Area Studies, like the CDP, rejected the view that deprivation was a reflection of inadequate personal and community attitudes and instead argued that deprivation was, simply, based on poverty. This poverty was, the studies argued, to a large degree caused by the declining and shifting job market in the inner cities and in particular was due to the closure and relocation of traditional inner city manufacturing firms. Inner area residents were left not only with fewer job opportunities but also with outdated skills, thus further reducing their chances of new employment.

The studies examined a wide range of issues affecting the inner city areas, from education to housing and urban planning, but their key themes remained those of industrial poverty and urban decay, clearly reflected in the 1977 White Paper. Nevertheless, as we shall see, central government failed to face up to the full implications of the analysis of deprivation put forward by the studies, as they had with the CDP before them. Urban policy, as manifested in the 1977 White Paper, was still to rely heavily on limited, pump-priming resources being directed to small, tightly defined areas of inner cities. The structuralist arguments were so powerful that government had been forced to shift its own position on inner cities policy, but only to a limited extent. For the ultimate implication of the structuralist account of urban deprivation would be that 'urban' policies themselves were an irrelevance, failing to address the underlying causes of inner city poverty, the national and international restructuring of the economy. An acceptance of this structuralist argument would have meant huge, costly and politically unacceptable programmes involving an examination of the possible effect on inner city deprivation of virtually all aspects of government activity, from economic policy to welfare benefits. Clearly, this was never going to be a political reality. Instead, the 'symbolic reassurance' of the 1977 White Paper prevailed, with a cut price programme being given the highest possible political profile, directed to a limited number of major urban conurbations.

Before examining the White Paper and the IAP in more detail, however, we need first to look at the other developments that were taking place within urban policy-making in the 1973–7 period.

Firstly, in November 1973, the Home Secretary announced the setting up of an Urban Deprivation Unit in the Home Office. The Home Secretary said of the Unit:

Essentially, it comprises two separate parts – a research organization and an organization for action. I have set in hand a wide-ranging study of the real nature of urban deprivation and the deeper problems underlying it. It is being conducted by a senior economic adviser who has a number of specially recruited staff to help him . . . the second part of the urban deprivation unit is the action part . . . in charge of a senior administrative civil servant. It is concerned with the immediate practical issues, with what we are doing now in government as a whole and what we might do to tackle the major problems. To this section will fall the job immediately of examining the need to bring together the various activities of Government Departments and to channel resources so far as possible to where they are most needed, so that we get much more co-ordinated positive discrimination in favour of these city problems. (House of Commons, Debate on Social Problems, 1 November 1973, cc. 340–1)

The Urban Deprivation Unit was set up specifically to develop a unified government response to the growing 'urban crisis'. In this, it had to overcome strong departmental resistance. The vying for position over the inner cities initiatives between key central government departments, particularly the DoE and the Home Office, and the lack of coordination between government departments became an increasing problem.

In the period after the 1974 election, the new Labour government began to shift the balance of power relating to inner city policy away from the Home Office and to the DoE. One of the first tasks of the Urban Deprivation Unit at the Home Office had been to set up the Comprehensive Community Programme (CCP), a scheme announced in the run-up to the 1974 election. The CCP was later transferred from Roy Jenkins at the Home Office to Peter Shore at the DoE. In addition, in September 1976, Peter Shore was given special responsibility for urban affairs, and was asked by the Prime Minister to chair a Cabinet Committee to co-ordinate the work of all government departments in this area. In the struggle for supremacy over the inner area policy, the DoE had clearly won by the time of the 1977 White Paper.

It is worth looking in some more detail at the CCP, given that this was explicitly designed to deal in a comprehensive way with the range of economic, social, physical and environmental problems of selected inner city areas. The CCP was meant to assist and inform a more unified government approach to urban deprivation. However, the Programme had a chequered history and, from the start, was embroiled in controversy (Spencer 1975).

The main objective of the CCP trials was to improve the management and coordination of existing city policy. In practice, the thrust of this was to foster corporate planning in local authorities, encouraging them to take an integrated and coordinated approach to their policies towards deprived urban areas as well as to their relations with central government and outside agencies, such as the private and voluntary sectors. This new corporate approach was also promoted in central government, with the new Urban Deprivation Unit providing a single focus to queries and policies concerning urban policy.

In practice this unified approach to the management of inner city policy was never really implemented. The first CCP trial, in Gateshead, was the only one to get under way and this was not until 1977. An important stumbling block for the Programme was its initial premise that deprivation occurred in small, identifiable urban areas. The pilot areas chosen in Wandsworth, Bradford, Gateshead and Motherwell were to concentrate on deprived areas of about 10,000 people, identified by indicators from the 1971 census. Alex Lyon, the Minister of State at the Home Office, had said that there were about ninety such deprived areas in the UK. However, as the CCP was being developed initial evidence from the CDP and Inner Area Studies was beginning to question the notion that deprivation was based in small pockets of multiply deprived people. As Lawless points out: 'Clearly the emphasis within central government was changing away from the idea that deprivation was based in small, identifiable urban localities, where it was sustained by clearly recognisable forces, towards more nationally oriented structuralist arguments relating to changing forces within employment, housing and education markets' (Lawless 1979, p. 91).

With the CDP and Inner Area Studies, together with the CCP and other initiatives, such as the Area Management Trials, the mid-1970s was clearly a period of great activity in the area of urban policy and analysis.

By September 1976, the Prime Minister had established a Cabinet Committee on the inner cities. Urban problems were being forced increasingly onto the national political agenda. The local elections in May of that year had seen the Labour Party, the 'traditional' party of the urban poor, being strongly challenged by the National Front in several large cities. One reason for this renewed interest in racist political parties was the expulsion of the Ugandan Asians by Idi Amin in 1971. Many of these came to the UK and settled particularly in Leicester, Bradford and Southall in London. In Leicester, this high level of immigration successfully provoked a racist backlash in the town. In the 1976 local elections a National Front candidate failed by only a few votes to get elected in one ward of the city. The gains made by the extreme far right shocked ministers, and forced them to reflect on the social divisions being fostered by the race issues specifically and by urban deprivation more generally.

On 17 September 1976, Peter Shore made a major speech in

Manchester in which he announced a new Labour government approach to inner cities. This speech heralded the beginnings of a new thrust of urban policy. formalized the following year by the White Paper *Policy for the Inner Cities* (Cmnd 6845). In April 1977, Shore announced the broad outline of the White Paper to the House of Commons. Following a ministerial review of the inner cities, he announced that the urban programme would be recast to cover economic, industrial and environment projects, as well as the traditional social projects. Drawing upon the available evidence, including the Inner Area Studies, he concluded that in the past too little attention had been paid to the economic development of the inner areas and that a new direction was needed.

Full details of these proposals were later set out in the White Paper, published in June of that year. The White Paper stated:

In summary, the Government's proposals are to:

(1) give a new priority in the main policies and programmes of government so that they contribute to a better life in the inner areas (paragraphs 44–8);
(2) strengthen the economies of inner areas as an immediate priority (paragraphs 49–58);
(3) secure a more unified approach to urban problems (paragraphs 59–62);
(4) recast the urban programme to cover economic and environmental projects and to increase its size (paragraphs 63–5);
(5) review and change policies on population movement (paragraphs 66–9);
(6) enter into special partnerships with the authorities – both districts and counties – of certain cities (paragraphs 70–82). (para. 41)

The White Paper, through its recasting of the traditional urban programme, brought into existence the Inner Area Programme, with its programme and partnership authorities. Although muddled in its objectives, the IAP was clearly built around a number of key themes; race (albeit implicit rather than explicit), area-based deprivation, strengthening the local economy, a partnership between local authorities and the residents of the inner city, and coordination of policy both in central government and in local authorities. These are continuing themes which will be picked up again and again throughout the book.

We will examine in more detail the IAP and its role as a poverty programme in the next section. First, however, we will trace the strands of urban policy from the late 1970s to the present, seeing how government thinking on the inner cities has developed. Shore's visionary initiatives were barely warming to their task when the arrival of Thatcherism provoked another major twist in the chronicle of urban policy.

Since 1979, the development of urban policy has continued to spawn regular initiatives punctuated by Cabinet Committees, Whitehall manoeuvring and, as always, prompted by recurrent social and particularly racial unrest in the cities. But under the Thatcher administrations urban policy has played to two insistent themes, privatization and centralization. The government announced it would be reviewing the urban programme soon after taking office in 1979. The new enthusiasm for the private sector was to be fully reflected in urban policy. The Secretary of State for the Environment, Michael Heseltine, announced the setting up of American-style Urban Development Corporations in 1979. The Minister for Local Government, Tom King, announced the following year that he thought 'voluntary groups can do more to tap the resources of the private sector, and free government money for the projects that would otherwise not go ahead'.

Heseltine insisted that consultation with local industry and commerce would be made a condition for urban programme grant, but the government wanted more than advice from the private sector. After the 1981 riots in Toxteth and elsewhere, Heseltine moved quickly to bus financiers around the inner cities, especially in Merseyside, and set up the Financial Institutions Group (FIG) comprising secondees from twenty-five institutions and companies. The urban development grants, aimed at rescuing derelict land, led to a flurry of activity, and high publicity displays like national garden festivals on urban wasteland. In the following three years, 165 projects received urban development grants, all but £78 million of the £400 million funding coming from the private sector. But more than a quarter of approved projects never got off the ground. The private sector remained unimpressed by the opportunities flourished under its nose to obtain both cheap investment opportunities and enterprise culture kudos from a few philanthropic gestures in the inner city. The FIG set up a new public company, Inner City Enterprises (ICE), but by 1985 ICE had raised funds for only six of the fifteen projects it had touted to the private sector, and one key backer, the National Westminster Bank, pulled out altogether.

By 1986, the urge to involve the private sector had moved on to a further stage. Urgent action was prompted by the 1985 disturbances in Handsworth Brixton and Tottenham. Legislation was announced to introduce a new form of grant, the urban regeneration grant, modelled on the urban development grant but paid directly to the private sector. The shift away from a comprehensive public sector policy for the inner cities since 1977 was now substantial.

This shift, however, did not mean reduced central government control and devolution to local authorities. On the contrary the complementary movement in policy in these years has been a proliferation of initiatives aimed at bypassing local authorities and strengthening Whitehall leverage over urban policy. In 1980, Chancellor of the Exchequer Geoffrey Howe announced the establishment of half a dozen enterprise zones, and a further nine were established at the end of 1982. In 1981, new and more *dirigiste* ministerial guidelines for Partnership and Programme authorities were issued identifying priorities and procedures. In 1983, the then Secretary of State for the Environment, Patrick Jenkin, announced that the Urban Development Programme, Urban Programme, and derelict land reclamation would be rationalized into a single block grant, cash limited for its capital elements.

The following years saw the multiplication of new measures generating a veritable alphabet soup of agencies and teams targeted at the inner cities, but all building on the network of bypasses now circulating round local authorities and providing a direct route from Whitehall to local areas. In 1985, Jenkin set up City Action Teams (CATs) in major conurbations, to knock heads together in an attempt to demonstrate decisive action. His party was rather spoilt, however, when the Association of Metropolitan Authorities pointed out that the councils in the five CAT areas had lost some £177 million in real terms in rate support grant since 1979/80. In the same year the Urban Programme Management Initiative (UPMI) was launched.

This came into operation in 1986/87 and was a response to the more general Financial Management Initiative in Whitehall. The UPMI aimed at ensuring closer central monitoring of urban programme expenditure. It constructed fifty output measures as

Whitehall, in the language now familiar among the civil servants involved, moved up the learning curve on the measurement of outputs on urban programme projects. Urban Development Corporations continued apace as their potential for the direct channelling of central government funds became increasingly attractive to a government locked in dispute with many local authorities, and seemingly with the whole apparatus of local government.

That local residents were complaining of the arrival of £2.5 million penthouses in London's Docklands, or that the CATs were, in the words of one sceptical former minister nothing more than 'a number of civil servants who meet once a month to exchange ideas' (Reg Freeson, Hansard, 6 March 1987, col. 1170), did nothing to dampen the enthusiasm of ministers for new initiatives. By 1987, however, the resulting confusion was beginning to cause some alarm. As the new Trade and Industry Minister, Kenneth Clarke, admitted, 'You've got city action teams, task forces, urban development corporations, enterprise zones, and all these kinds of schemes and grants, regeneration grants, estate action to restore old houses – I could go on producing an endless list' (*Guardian*, 29 July 1987). For a government committed to rolling back the frontiers of the state, urban policy had become anfractuously quangoid. As one seasoned commentator summed up this process, 'This proliferation of semi-autonomous and/or centrally accountable institutions and the parallel dilution in the role and function of local authority partnership and programme authorities represents a major shift in the interest and power structure within inner cities policy' (Stewart 1987, p. 8). Within Whitehall too the centre of gravity for inner cities policy was shifting away from environment and increasingly towards industrial and employment policy. When Lord David Young of Graffham and Kenneth Clarke moved to Trade and Industry after the 1987 election they took with them the leadership of inner city policy under the direct supervision of the Prime Minister, herself now chair of yet another Cabinet Committee on the inner cities.

One of the most interesting of these developments has been the Task Force scheme. Representing in part this shift in the balance of power within as well as towards Whitehall, this scheme was created in early 1986 by Kenneth Clarke, then Minister for Employment under the ubiquitously influential Lord Young. Initially eight employment task forces were set up in selected areas with loud fanfares about their ability to cut red tape and replace some of the more nonsensical excesses of some local authorities with serious approaches to training and employment. Further areas were added later. One of the first areas selected was in Leicester, the city we look at more closely in Part Two of this book. We can look briefly here at the experience of the task force in Leicester.

The task force in Leicester met with outright and vociferous opposition from the City Council. As the local evening paper described it, 'The little task force must sometimes feel as if they were invading the Falklands in a rowing boat, so fierce is the resentment that has been whipped up against them' (*Leicester Mercury*, 29 June 1987). The task force landed in June 1986, and rapidly set up a local base. Several highly publicized visits by Kenneth Clarke followed. One immediate local response was the establishment of a shadow task force by voluntary and community groups in the area, which though not entirely representative of the diversity of ethnic minority groups locally, did articulate local suspicions about the government's initiative.

After a year of operation the task force had given support to eight projects, including a grant to the Industrial Society to run enterprise courses for young people, money to assist bricklayers on an IAP project to get City and Guilds qualifications, money to buy a building for a textile arts centre running as an MSC project, and transport for a workshop centre. To the irritation of the City Council most of these projects were already receiving support from the Council, through the IAP, or were prevented from doing so by DoE rules. In its frustration the City Council drew a contrast between the increasingly dead hand of the DoE on the IAP and the task force's claim that it could operate with the minimum of bureaucracy and the maximum urgency.

The general shift in policy since 1979, then, has seen a steady growth in central government intervention in local urban policy via the construction of a plethora of initiatives bypassing the control of local authorities. At the same time urban policy has become increasingly an adjunct of employment policy as displayed by recurrent though less than entirely successful attempts to persuade, coerce or bribe the private sector to play a larger role, and by the steady advance of Employment and Trade and Industry as the homes of urban policy in Whitehall.

Conclusion: the IAP as a poverty programme

Our examination of the early poverty programmes in Chapters 1 and 2 has highlighted a number of common factors in both American and British programmes. Firstly, they have been directed towards a variety of 'urban' problems which are seen to stem from the multiple disadvantages or deprivations that are suffered by certain communities in inner city or ghetto areas of older towns. Positive discrimination is seen as the way to deal with these problems, through public programmes which favour these areas. It is claimed for positive discrimination that it can direct resources accurately and quickly to the areas of greatest need. In contrast to a system of universal benefits, which is seen as costly and inefficient, positive discrimination offers the opportunity to delimit without stigmatizing, being selective on an area rather than a personal basis. In a time of financial stringency there are obvious attractions for a scheme that can claim to be cheap, efficient and effective.

Secondly, they have sought to tackle these problems through a series of special projects, designed at the local level to meet the specific needs of the area. The relationship between these special projects and the main programme activities of central and local government is a distant one. Whilst it is hoped that these projects can have a demonstration effect, exploring new ways of tackling old problems, these programmes have been both additional and peripheral to the main activities of government agencies.

Thirdly, the programmes have had a particular style of funding, central government providing the majority of finance, usually 75–90 per cent, the remainder being found by local government. Funding of projects is usually on a short-term basis. The justification for this form of finance is that it offers the combination of central direction and local innovation.

Fourthly, the programmes have included a commitment to public involvement, which could take many forms, ranging from consultation in defining needs and priorities in an area through to full participation in the designing and implementation of projects. The stated aim of this involvement is as an end itself, helping to overcome the apathy and alienation of inner city residents which is identified as a problem by the state.

This examination of the early poverty programmes has revealed a number of contradictions between their stated objectives and their performance. Firstly, despite the rhetoric of waging a 'war on poverty', the resources committed ensure that it is no more than an extremely localized skirmish. If a full-scale battle was to be fought then it would surely require the employment of main programme battalions. Whilst it is hoped that these special programmes will have an effect, their impact is most visible as a low cost, high profile political demonstration. The political motivations behind these special programmes are confirmed by their spatial bias, directed specifically at urban areas. If the concern was to tackle the problem of poverty then there is no justification for this urban bias. This bias can be explained, however, if the real objective of these programmes is to deal with the threat of racial unrest and street violence. Seen in the context of fiscal crisis poverty programmes offer the state an opportunity to maintain consent at a low cost in areas where the potential for disorder is greatest.

At this stage it is worth reminding ourselves of the main characteristics of the IAP as a poverty programme, highlighting the contradictory and frequently ambiguous nature of not only its theoretical approach but also of its internal structures. In essence we argue that each aspect of the IAP (or any poverty programme) is open to two diametrically opposed readings based on two alternative theories of the state.

1. *The objectives of the IAP.*   The government claims that the IAP is an attempt to tackle the problems of urban deprivation that occur in the centre of our older cities. Yet poverty has no special urban characteristics, nor is it solely concentrated in the inner city. Both the timing of new poverty programmes and their location support the radical interpretation developed in this book which sees the IAP as a high profile, low cost political programme aimed at securing consent amongst disadvantaged groups and reducing the likelihood of public disorder. Whilst the threat to public order is rarely made explicit, the interrelated concerns for the decline in community spirit, the rise in racial tension and the need for tough but sensitive policing provide the thinly disguised hidden agenda for the IAP.

2. *An area-based policy.*   The justification for an area-based programme is that the problem being addressed is concentrated in certain areas, affording the opportunity for a narrowly

focused policy of positive discrimination in favour of that area. However, as there is no such concentration of poverty, at either a national or local level, an alternative reading is again suggested. As Chapters 1 and 2 have shown the factor which is concentrated in urban areas is the potential for public disorder.

3. *A small-scale problem.*   In comparison to the main programme budgets of central and local government, the resources devoted to poverty programmes are limited. The main reason given for this paucity of resources is that the problem itself, while serious, is limited in scale. Thus the problems of urban deprivation are contained within the inner urban areas of a few local authorities, who are the 'natural agencies' to deal with them. From a radical perspective the problems of urban deprivation are neither small in scale nor concentrated in central localities, nor capable of local resolution. Rather the scale of resources is dictated by the fiscal concerns of the state, which seeks to restrict the money spent on social expenses, being that part of the state expenditure whose aim is to secure consent.

4. *An innovative programme.*   The IAP, like other poverty programmes, places a strong emphasis on innovation. Its resources are not meant to be used to finance 'more of the same' but rather to set up experimental schemes to test new approaches. Whilst limited in resources, the claim for the greater relevance and impact of these programmes rests in the ability to innovate, with their lessons being transferred to other public programmes. As we shall see in Part Two, there has been little innovation or public learning in the IAP, with both the regulations governing the preparation of the IAP and the cutbacks in main programme expenditure undermining any attempts at experimentation. Rather, the novelty of the IAP presents the chance for political publicity that would not have arisen without the creation of a new programme. Whilst there is nothing new about the IAP, it offers the opportunity for symbolic reassurance whereby a problem is named, contained and under the control of this 'new' initiative.

5. *A programme of projects.*   The format of the IAP is typical of other poverty programmes in the reliance it places on a series of special projects to deliver its impact. New projects are seen as providing the best vehicle for small, one-off innovatory schemes. Being locally designed to meet local needs, they offer the opportunity of direct and precise intervention. The indi-

vidual projects are expected to conform to an overall strategy, with the programme, in total, adding up to more than the sum of its component parts.

In practice, as we shall see in Chapter 4, the constraints on policy-making are such as to restrict the opportunity to develop an IAP strategy at the local level. The IAP process becomes an annual allocation exercise with the 'programme' reduced to an *ad hoc* collection of projects. In terms of the political impact of a poverty programme, projects offer a means of creating a large number of beneficiaries at a low cost and of directing political patronage to key target groups (Chapter 5).

6. *Joint financing*. Poverty programmes are jointly funded by central and local government. In the cases of the IAP 75 per cent of the costs are met by central government and the remaining 25 per cent by local authorities. The rationale for this arrangement is found in two factors. Firstly, the urgency of the situation, often portrayed as a crisis, defines a local problem as of national concern. Secondly, due to the experimental nature of the programme and the national significance of the results, local authorities are to receive support for projects during their initial trial period.

Alternatively, the joint funding arrangements can be seen to offer the dominant partner both the means and the motive for control. Central government is in a position to impose conditions upon local authorities, who, in turn, can control voluntary projects because of the nature of financial dependency. In addition, the (alleged) innovatory nature of the IAP is used to legitimize the monitoring and control of both programmes and projects.

These contradictory interpretations of the programmes we have described in Chapters 1 and 2 are summarized in Table 1.

To conclude, Chapters 1 and 2 have traced the political economy of the 'urban problem' and the schemes initiated in response to this problem. We have shown how urban policy has developed, particularly under Conservative governments since 1979, further into an industrial and economic policy and with an increased emphasis on bypassing local government structures. This shift in the approach and organization of urban policy adds depth to the question we have posed in the first two chapters about the

Table 1   *The contradictory nature of poverty programmes*

Feature	Official justification	Hidden agenda
1. Objective	To tackle urban poverty	To maintain public order and consent
2. An area-based policy	Poverty is concentrated in certain areas	The threat to public order is urban based
3. A small-scale problem	Urban poverty is small in scale, to be tackled by local programme	Poverty is widespread, requiring expensive national action
4. Innovation	Public learning	Symbolic reassurance
5. A programme of projects	Direct help to local problems	Vehicle for political patronage
6. Joint funding	Experimentation requires joint central and local government initiative	Experimentation justifies control

relation of urban initiatives to poverty programmes. The grand designs and ambitions behind the visionary schemes described in Chapter 1, and the more prosaic but detailed initiatives outlined earlier in this chapter, now seem far removed from the fundamental attack on urban deprivation they all would claim as their rationale.

Poverty programmes can only succeed if designed to tackle either or both of two issues. Firstly, they can directly address the problem of income distribution through the labour market, by tackling incomes or employment policy, by fiscal measures aimed at a more progressive tax system, or through income maintenance programmes. Secondly, poverty can be tackled through the provision of collective services at cost to the public purse which substantially reduces the effective cost of living for low income households, and increases their disposable incomes.

No poverty programme conceived as an attack on the problems of the cities has addressed either of these approaches, which would in practice, of course, have to be complementary rather than alternative. On the contrary all such initiatives, driven by fear of urban unrest and targeted at maximum display, have left largely untouched the underlying problems of those who live in the inner cities. A case, one might be tempted to conclude, of fiddling the figures while homes burn. In Chapter 3 we examine the contextual economic and political imperatives which have ensured this pattern.

3   The IAP: fiscal crisis and symbolic reassurance

In the previous chapters we described how successive governments in Britain and America developed poverty programmes in response to the problems of urban areas, and suggested that the political energy behind these programmes derived from fear of violence, specifically in a racial context. In this chapter we see that in the British context also this fear of the 'ungovernability' of the poor, the blacks and the dispossessed in the inner cities was a key factor behind the introduction of the IAP, particularly in the context of fiscal crisis. Fiscal crisis occurs when the state's expenditure rises faster than its revenue, and during such a crisis the ability of the state to buy off urban unrest via public expenditure is limited. The state needs cheap but politically potent and highly visible programmes to quell such urban problems: the IAP can be situated firmly within this context.

The chapter examines the role of urban fiscal crisis in the introduction of the IAP and goes on to analyse the role of the IAP as symbolic reassurance. It then examines the degree of disparity between the political commitment to the Programme and the actual financial resources available. Finally, the developments around the IAP in the 1980s are discussed, and we begin to examine the relationship between urban left-wing councils and the Thatcher government over urban policy.

What kind of crisis?

The IAP was introduced in 1977 against a background of fiscal crisis. It followed the dramatic shift in economic policy engineered by Denis Healey's 1975 budget and the 1976 International Monetary Fund (IMF) 'rescue package' which finally finished any attempt to 'spend our way of out of a recession', as Labour Prime

Minister James Callaghan famously and scathingly described earlier policies in his 1976 speech to the Party conference.

This was a key issue behind the urban problem as it was perceived in the late 1970s, but there were two other important issues related to fiscal crisis: the 'ungovernability' problem of the inner cities and the relations between central and local government. We need to consider these issues in turn to understand the background to the IAP.

Fiscal crisis was a term first used by O'Connor (1973) to describe and explain the state's expenditure rising faster than its revenue. O'Connor argued that the state has two principal and often contradictory functions: accumulation (securing the conditions for the expansion of private profit) and legitimation (securing the conditions of social harmony to permit this accumulation to continue).

In financing its services the state experiences two long-term problems. Firstly, there has been a rise in relative costs in the public sector: 'Because the social services (like all services) are very labour intensive, and because there is less possibility of raising productivity to offset higher wages, the relative costs of providing them rise year by year' (Gough 1979, p. 85). Secondly, over recent decades there has been an absolute increase in state expenditure due to both increased pressure for new and improved services (e.g. higher education) and to a rise in the dependent population: spending on social services needs to grow at around 2 per cent a year just to take account of the ageing population.

The tendency for state expenditure to grow over time is shown in the public expenditure figures. In 1911, state expenditure in the UK at factor cost was 12.7 per cent of GNP. This had risen to 44.9 per cent in 1951 and to 57.9 per cent by 1975 (quoted in Gough 1979, p. 77). The ability of the state to raise sufficient revenue to finance its expenditure is put under strain during an economic recession.

Whilst the state provides the infrastructure and subsidies necessary to support the accumulation of private capital, it does not gain the benefits directly, only what it is able to recoup in taxation. In a recession, when arguably both the need to restructure the economy and the demands on welfare payments are greatest, the contraction of the economic base causes pressure on the state's revenue, producing a fiscal crisis.

Public expenditure has, of course, continued to grow. Despite the climactic recession of the early 1980s, with the public sector borrowing requirement rising to over £11 billion before the 1983 election, the Thatcher government, though committed to rolling back the frontiers of the state, presided over a rise in public expenditure of 14 per cent between 1979 and 1986 (Hills 1987; Robinson 1986). This disguises, however, three shifts directly relevant to our discussion here.

Firstly, there has been a substantial shift in public expenditure away from many key welfare areas, particularly those administered at local level, and, most dramatically, housing. In the period 1979–86 housing expenditure was reduced in real terms by 55 per cent, contrasted with a rise in defence expenditure of 28 per cent (Hills 1987). Where there had been 180,000 housing starts in 1975/6, a decade later the figure was just 36,000. The total rented stock held by local authorities in England fell from 5.157 million in 1978 to 4.579 million in 1987 (HC Hansard, 29 June 1987, WA col. 41–2). Central government subsidies to local authority housing were cut by nearly 80 per cent between 1979/80 and 1984/5, a drop of £900 million, and it became increasingly common to talk of the 'residualization' of public sector housing as poorly maintained estates became isolated sectors containing concentrations of low income, unemployed and increasingly embittered tenants not remotely excited by the growth in opportunities to buy their rented property.

Secondly, shifts in public expenditure meant a marked reduction in public investment. The familiar litany of complaints about peeling paintwork, squalid school toilets or ancient hospital buildings reflects the fact that 'since 1981 gross public investment has only just kept ahead of depreciation and there has hardly been any net investment at all' (Hills 1987, p. 98). The services affected, of course, are just those most used by the urban poor, and most prominent in the relationship between local authorities and their residents. By 1983/4 local capital expenditure was only 49 per cent of its peak in 1974 (Page 1986).

The third factor is the shift in the balance of public expenditure between central and local authorities. We examine later the specific aspects of this related to the urban programme. The point to note is the rising proportion of local expenditure which has had to be raised from local rates. The rate support grant fell as a proportion of local expenditure from 66.5 per cent in 1975/6 to 47 per cent in 1985/6. Yet alongside this reduction in central government funding has been a legislative regime increasing central control over local expenditure. This is buttressed by a widening range of specific and supplementary grants for particular government-approved programmes, together with a general centralist tendency facilitated by the replacement of local functions by activities within the control of central bodies like the Manpower Service Commission (MSC) (Ward and Williams 1986). Of course there has been a general drift in the loss of local functions exercised by local authorities since the 1930s – water, health and poor relief being major examples. But in the recent advance of attempts to reduce the burden of rates and diminish the autonomy of troublesome burghers, reductions in central financing have been crucial. By 1987/8 the accumulated reduction in rate support grant since 1978/9 was £3,896.2 million at 1987/8 prices. This compares pointedly with the £3,500 million spent on all urban programmes by the DoE over the same period. (HC Hansard, 29 June 1987, WA col. 43, and 1 April 1987, WA col. 544).

Thus while public expenditure has been forced to rise under the pressures of demography, unemployment and the relative price effect, attempts to balance the books of the fiscal crisis have turned expenditure massively away from those areas of public services most important to lower income groups in the worst hit localities of urban decline. Inevitably then the key site of struggle over the fiscal crisis has been the inner city on both sides of the Atlantic, as shown most dramatically in New York (1975–8) and Liverpool (1984). Its classic symptoms are widening disparities between revenues and expenditures on the one hand, and rising demands for municipal services on the other.

Large cities are so politically important, and such a source of potential or actual social unrest, that governments will always be forced to treat seriously the developments affecting its main urban areas:

Urban areas are critically important sites at which both economic growth and political integration are organized. Government structures in urban areas must therefore perform key functions both to support urban economic processes and to promote the political integration of the urban population. On the one hand, urban governments must be responsive to the infrastructural and service requirements of capital accumulation, and to changes in these requirements generated by economic growth. On the other hand, they must also manage political participation among the masses of urban population who do not control capital accumulation and may not benefit from it either. (Friedland *et al.* 1977, p. 449)

Thus the state's record on both its accumulation and legitimation functions will to a large extent depend on its performance in urban centres and in particular on the activities of local government – the local state. The history of the relationship between central and local government sees a mixture of legal powers and financial controls being used by central government in order to secure its own objectives. The problem for central government is one of control. Over the years the services of local government have grown in relative importance and play a crucial role in influencing the life chances and standard of living of the majority of people in the country. However, not only are its services important but local government is also both more visible and accessible to the populace than is central government, making it much more open to local political pressure. In Friedland *et al.*'s terms, local government becomes the 'shock absorber' of the upheavals produced by the national political economy.

As 'shock absorbers', urban local authorities have opted to increase their expenditure on public services, rather than run the risk of electoral unpopularity or, at worst, civil disobedience:

The tensions which might otherwise take the form of direct struggles between business, industry and finance on the one hand, and workers and consumers on the other hand, take the form instead of escalating demands on municipal agencies – for jobs, services, contracts, tax concessions – with the result that municipal activities and budgets expand, while municipal revenues are reduced. As a consequence, periods of potential social and class conflict become instead periods of fiscal strains. (Friedland *et al.*, p. 450)

As central and local governments have different responsibilities and are subject to different political pressures, there exists the potential for disputes over both the type and extent of public services administered at the local level. Central government is under pressure from both business and financial interests to reduce public expenditure. While local authorities face immediate and direct pressure to maintain and improve their services, central government has been under pressure to reduce public expenditure, and, under the Thatcher administration, limiting public expenditure has been an overt objective of national government.

The greatest divergence between the interests of the two levels of the state occurs in the inner city where the economy is declining yet the demand for public services is expanding. The relationship between central and local government, particularly in the large urban areas of Britain has of course changed dramatically since 1979, with Thatcherite monetarism at the national level coupled with the election of urban local authorities committed to explicitly socialist policies, achieved through increased rate revenues. As we shall see, by the mid-1980s, urban fiscal crisis had reached a new state, and with it the IAP was beginning to play a subtly different role. Firstly, however, we must look at the way in which the IAP was used in a symbolic manner.

The IAP as symbolic reassurance

A central aspect of the IAP is its importance as a legitimation exercise, offering the government the opportunity to name, contain and redefine the urban problem, then to demonstrate its commitment to tackling the issue.

By launching a new initiative the government gained useful publicity. The novelty of the IAP made it newsworthy and offered politicians the opportunity to be publicly identified with an initiative that was both progressive and innovative. The IAP had a high political profile. Certain ministers, notably Peter Shore and Reg Freeson, were closely associated with it, addressing conferences, public meetings and then chairing partnership committees.

However, the significance of this innovatory programme went beyond novelty value and the publicity that followed. The new programme offered the state the chance to redefine a 'problem' and reassure the public that the situation was under control. Thus the IAP became an exercise in symbolic reassurance. The new programme initiated both a naming and categorizing process. To an extent the label that is attached to a problem determines how it is viewed, which in turn determines the action required to tackle it.

The importance of linguistics in shaping the response to social problems was outlined by Murray Edelman in his book, *Political Language: Words that Succeed and Policies that Fail* (1977). Edelman argued that it is the linguistic structures and references that are used to *describe* issues that determine the way that people *perceive* them. Thus, if the debate about poverty is seen through the concept of 'scrounging' a whole referential context is constructed that affects both the way poverty is perceived and the solutions that follow (Golding and Middleton 1982). Edelman argues that it is the defining of this referential context that is of prime importance in the debate on social policy:

Political and ideological debate consists very largely of efforts to win acceptance of a particular categorisation of an issue in the face of competing efforts on behalf of a different one; but because participants are likely to see it as a dispute either about facts or about individual values, the linguistic (that is, social) basis of perceptions is usually unrecognized. (p. 25)

It has been through the IAP that the government has made a crucial intervention in determining the cognitive structures that have defined debate around the 'urban crisis'. There have been two, conflicting, negative views of the inner city. The first is that of the inner city as a hopeless wasteland with pathological problem households living in a blighted area. The second is that of the inner city of the 'residuum', the dangerous classes, riotous in nature, involved in an anti-social underworld of petty crime and vandalism. The White Paper drifted uneasily between these two views of the inner city, unclear about which problem it wanted to solve. The 'moral panic' contained in these views has been explored by Stuart Hall, who argued that the issue of mugging united the themes of crime, race and the ghetto, and included:

the involvement of blacks and drugs in crime; the expansion of the black ghettos, coupled with the growth of black social and political militancy; the threatened crisis and collapse of the cities; the crime panic and the appeal to 'law and order' . . . These topics and themes were not as clearly separated as these headings imply. They tended, in public discussion, to come together into a general scenario of conflict and crisis. In an important sense the image of 'mugging' came ultimately to contain and express them all. (Hall *et al*. 1978, p. 329)

Hall and his colleagues argue that in the public's mind the mugger posed not just a physical threat but, more seriously, a moral danger by attacking the core values associated with the British way of life. It was to counter this negative view of the ghetto and its inhabitants that the inner city initiative attempted to substitute a set of positive images.

The referential context of the IAP draws on a number of key concepts that are central to British cultural and political traditions combining to create a positive view of the British way of life that was to revive the inner city. The core concepts underpinning the inner cities initiative were those of stability, self-help and common purpose that are considered in turn below.

Stability

In place of the shifting, rootless nether world of the ghetto peopled by a nomad race of criminals, *Policy for the Inner Cities* substituted the image of community, stable both in the sense of its people and their values. The White Paper describes how the flight of investment and jobs to the suburbs had left the inner city to decay. What was needed was a new balance between the inner cities and the surrounding region. A deliberate effort is needed to reduce, and possibly in some cases to end, the loss of people and jobs from the cities as a whole and the inner cities in particular.

The emotional appeal of this return to the inner city was strong, with Peter Shore talking in biblical language of 'reversing the engines of exodus'. Certainly for the Labour Party the IAP represented a 'Passport to Pimlico', a return to its homeland, both geographically (to the terraced streets of the inner city) and politically (to the Party's traditional concerns for urban poverty). The appeal of this return to the inner city was more than just an electoral one for the Labour Party. It touched on a raw nerve, a collective guilt about the persistent inequalities of the post-war world that the Labour Party had helped to shape. Whilst growth had produced a rise in general material wealth, the benefits were not enjoyed by all. The inner city areas had lost their people and, through redevelopment, lost their old homes and their communities. Whilst the young, the skilled and the mobile left the inner city for new jobs in the new towns they left behind the less affluent or mobile to suffer the traumas of development.

Tower blocks became symbols of an uncaring society, of loneliness and isolation of communities literally turned on their end. The alienation and apathy highlighted in the White Paper was specifically the antagonism of the inner city residents towards the public authorities (usually Labour controlled) that had destroyed their areas in the name of progress.

The vision in the White Paper of a return to the inner city thus contained more than merely a geographical switch in the pattern of investment. Rather, at a symbolic level, it represented a return to its roots for the Labour Party.

Partnership

One of the negative images of the ghetto is as a place of conflict, be it on the level of individual violence, the mugger, or at the mass level, with a riot. The inner city initiative sought to neutralize this image of conflict by constructing an image of harmony. The IAP was to be based around the concept of partnership, in which the agencies of government worked with the public to achieve the common goal of reviving the inner city. As we argue later, the ambition of partnership was unrealistic given the fact that the inner city represents, in geographical terms, a conflict between competing interests. The inner city and its residents were not poor as a result of an inevitable ageing process: the inner city had declined due to the investment decisions of private and public institutions.

Given the realities of this conflict (between central and local government, between city and county, between labour and capital, etc.) how could a strategy be developed based on partnership? The answer is that partnership was a powerful symbol, even if politically a non-starter. The image of partnership was one of a community pulling togeher. In an inner city context it draws on diffuse memories of the Blitz when cheerful Cockneys remained undaunted by the bombs because their spirit could not be broken. This is a key concept in the British way of life, a nation of individuals that come together in a time of crisis, forget their differences and pull together towards a common goal. That the IAP should enrol the war-time spirit was not coincidential. It was the collective experience of the war-time years that produced the Labour victory in 1945 and it was just such a revival that the IAP itself was aimed at producing.

Self-help

The final core image for the IAP was that of self-help, which in turn summoned up its own component images. Firstly, by suggesting that the poor should help themselves by their own effort it stresses the values of work. Contrasted with the view of the work-shy scroungers of the ghetto is the positive image that places the responsibility for inner city revival on the efforts of the residents themselves. Secondly, self-help implies a concern for individual conduct. The White Paper talks of 'a collective deprivation in some areas that affects all the residents . . . It arises from a pervasive sense of decay and neglect which affects the whole area, through a decline in community spirit . . . All this may make it harder for people to maintain their personal standards' (para. 17). Clearly the IAP is seeking to combat this social malaise by a return to respectability via a path familiar to George Orwell and Richard Hoggart, getting back to the decent working class. Again the image involved is essentially a conservative one with the return to the inner city reflecting a return to a mythical past.

Drawing the images of stability, of partnership and self-help together we see an attempt to mobilize core values in the British way of life, to provide a new referential context to the inner city that could counteract the negative image of the ghetto. These images are summarized in Table 2.

Table 2 *Counter-images of the ghetto and the inner city*

Ghetto	Inner city
American	English
Conflict	Community
Black	White
Shifting	Stable
Crime	Work
Decay	Renewal
Neglect	Care
Dependence	Self-help

Complementary to this ideological and rhetorical aspect of the IAP is a real shift in the nature of the populations served by such programmes. Analytically this has been identified in recent years as a growth of sectoral cleavages in the social structure of urban populations, in which the traditional ties of class rooted in work – the relations of production – are increasingly replaced by collectivities based on consumption of such services as housing, transport or education. These new identities profoundly influence such behaviour as voting and produce what is in effect a dual system of politics, class based at national level, sectorally based around consumption at local level. One does not necessarily replace the other, but 'consumption positions cannot be assimilated into or explained in terms of occupational class' (Dunleavy 1979, p. 417; see also Dunleavy and Husbands 1985).

The debate engendered by this notion has been lively and extensive, and we cannot here enter the lists of the very large literature produced by the renaissance of urban social theory in the last decade (for a brief overview see Flynn (1986)). However, it is clear that in examining the power of rhetorical bases to the IAP we should be aware that such rhetoric is addressed to populations whose traditional political and social ties may well be subject to a number of cross-cutting and complex movements. This will be important in Part Two when we examine the relationship between the Programme and the voluntary sector.

Where's the money to come from? IAP and the changing economic climate

In examining the IAP as a response to fiscal crisis we have seen how, as an exercise in symbolic reassurance, it supports the legitimation objectives of the state. However, legitimation had to be achieved within the constraints of existing budgets. In this section we examine, at the general level, how the IAP enables the state to reorder its *priorities* for public spending in favour of urban trouble spots without actually increasing its *level* of expenditure.

In this debate it is important to differentiate both between the different levels of the state, central and local, and also the various interests that compete within each level. Also, in the years since the introduction of the IAP there have been major changes in political control at various levels of the state and these have produced alterations in policies and priorities.

The IAP can be seen as a response by the central state to fiscal crisis on two specific counts; the resources made available and the spatial direction of expenditure. These will be considered in turn.

The resources for the IAP

When first announced, there was considerable uncertainty about what scale of initiative the IAP represented. The White Paper (House of Commons 1977) stated that 'The time has now come to give the inner areas an explicit priority in social and economic policy, even at a time of particular stringency in public resources' (para. 3). However, what in practice was to be the balance between 'priority' and 'stringency'? Was the IAP to be a major government initiative or merely another in a long line of cut-price poverty programmes? Whilst attention focused on resource commitment to provide the answers, there was considerable ambiguity about what the level of financial commitment was. Nowhere was the IAP more vague than in its references to resources. Finance for the inner area was to come from three sources: special projects funded through the IAP grant aid, additional allocation from the rate support grant and finally from the redirection of main programme expenditure. These three categories will be examined below, highlighting the disparaties that emerged between promise and performance.

Grant aid

The government recast the UP such that Partnership and Programme authorities gained direct assistance via grant aid, received through the IAP.

Thus in 1979/80, the first year of the IAP, £125 million was made available to the twenty-two recently designated IAP authorities, which represented some £13.70 per head of their population. As such, it could hardly be counted as a major attack on the problems of urban poverty. An additional reservation was that this £125 million did not represent any increase in overall public spending as it was 'redirected' from the existing budgets of central government departments. Whilst the inner area authorities gained from the IAP, this was at the expense of their non-IAP counterparts. Thus the IAP resources represented a reordering of priorities rather than an increased commitment to public spending.

As such there were clear limitations on the contribution that could be expected from the grant aid element of the IAP.

The major resources for the IAP were to come from its two other sources:

Rate support grant

In 1977, approximately two-thirds of the monies spent by local government came from central government through the rate support grant (RSG). Changes in this grant were to play a major part in the resource strategy for the IAP. In the 1977 White Paper, it was stated that the grant was 'bound to be the prime source of Government funds for helping the regeneration of the inner areas' (para. 47). As part of the inner city initiative

> more account has been taken of the problems of urban authorities and a greater share of needs element has been allocated to London and the metropolitan areas. The Government intend to ensure that full account continues to be taken of the needs of authorities with severe urban problems. It will be up to all authorities to use their allocations of rate support grant to assist the revival of the inner areas. (para. 47)

In practice, whilst IAP authorities did benefit initially from changes in the support grant, the Conservative government, elected in May 1979, had different priorities both for the level and direction of public spending which have had serious implications for the concept of the IAP. In the case of public expenditure cuts, it is no longer possible to talk of a partnership between central and local government, or of any explicit priority for the inner city.

Redirection of main programme expenditure

One of the lessons from the Inner Area Studies was the importance of a 'total approach' to the problems of the inner city. This meant using the main policies of both central and local government departments to tackle the problems at hand. In *Policy for the Inner Cities* it was recommended that these main programmes be brought into an overall strategy for the inner city, with each containing an 'inner area dimension and priority' (para. 45).

The implications of this policy for local authorities were enormous, for not only was the DoE to redirect its main programme activities, such as the Housing Investment Programme (HIP), in favour of the inner city but so too would other departments, like the Department of Education, Department of Employment, Department of Health and Social Security, Department of Industry and the Home Office. Indeed, a considerable amount of space is devoted in the White Paper to outlining how this redirection was to be achieved, and it was this paper commitment that gave the inner city initiative its initial credibility.

The bending of main programmes was not to be restricted to central government departments: 'Local authorities, for their part, can do a great deal to redirect their policies to give assistance to inner areas and to bring about a more co-ordinated approach. There is scope for making better use of resources and for pursuing policies of positive discrimination' (para. 46). In the event, very little came of redirection, at either national or local level. There was a notable fall off in interest and commitment to the IAP from other departments, with the DoE finding it increasingly difficult to maintain their interest. This was finally killed off by the incoming Conservative government whose alternative philosophies on public spending provided civil servants with more important things to worry about; not least of all their own futures! At the local level the changing climate for public expenditure has also undermined the credibility of the IAP and *de facto* relegated the issue of redirection to the filing cabinets.

More means less: money in the IAP after 1979

The election of the Conservative government in May 1979 saw a marked change in policy towards the IAP in particular and to local government and public expenditure in general. For the incoming government, the priority which overrode all other considerations was the need to reduce the fiscal strain on the state, in line with its monetarist policies aimed at cutting inflation. Public expenditure had to be reduced even if this entailed political conflict. Drastic public expenditure cuts brought a sharp rise in unemployment and then riots in 1981, predictably in the inner city.

These years marked a change in direction for the IAP. Following a lengthy period of review, approval was given to its continuation, although with a different emphasis. Priority was to be given to restructuring the economy of the inner city, with economic and capital expenditure favoured over social consumption projects, such as in recreation, education or housing. At the same time a series of new initiatives were launched to help private enterprise in the inner area. Urban development grants were made available to encourage large capital projects in the inner city, funded jointly by private and public finance. Also a number of enterprise zones were set up with which firms would receive preferential treatment as regards issues such as rates, whilst a number of public controls were relaxed, for example in the field of planning. But whilst the state was 'getting off the back' of the entrepreneur, cutting the red tape and giving him the green light, it was swiftly climbing on to the back of local government, where the lights were switched to a permanent red. Two developments are notable here; the change in the allocation of resources for urban initiatives and the growth in the population covered.

General expenditure on the urban programme can look impressive in round figures. Between 1978/9 and 1987/8 the DoE urban programmes cumulatively cost in excess of £3500 million. But annual figures are relatively small in the context of overall public expenditure, and as Table 3 shows, have declined in real terms since 1983. The traditional urban programme was cut by over a third in real terms between 1982 and 1986, though the higher profile activities in the partnership and programme authorities have not suffered as much. In 1987/8 the urban programme was cut again, by 1.5 per cent in real terms, to £324 million. From

Table 3   *The Urban Programme 1979/80 to 1986/7*[a,c]

Year	Total (£m)	Adjusted Total (£m)[b]	Totals include		
			Traditional Urban Programme	Partnership	Programme
1979/80	175	210	30	100	32
1980/81	202	202	33	116	47
1981/82	215	193	42	118	50
1982/83	295	246	47	143	77
1983/84	310	246	53	133	86
1984/85	320	244	47	131	97
1985/86	317	228	44	121	99
1986/87	317	220	37	123	97

Notes:
[a] Source: adapted from House of Common's Library Research Division, Reference Sheet No. 86/13, October 1986, p. 19.
[b] Figures adjusted using the GDP deflator, 1980 = 100.
[c] Figures include the 25 per cent contributed by local authorities to urban programme expenditures.

that year bids were no longer invited for the Traditional Urban Programme, to allow for 'a substantial improvement in the targetting and management of the Urban Programme' (that is concentrating resources in IAP authorities).

Much spending ends up as an array of penny packages. By 1984, with 12 000 schemes running, only 20 per cent of capital and 5 per cent of current schemes cost more than £50 000 (Committee of Public Accounts 1986). In the context of urban spending, too, this is small beer. In 1984/5, when the services in aggregate provided by local authorities cost over £45 000 million the urban programme cost £320 million, or well under a hundredth of the first figure. In that year local authority budgeted expenditure for partnership and programme authorities was £3500 million, while urban programme resources for those areas were allocated at £170 million (Committee of Public Accounts 1986).

While, as Table 3 shows, the IAP is a relatively low cost initiative, it is also dwarfed by the scale of cuts in available resources in many areas. Table 4 shows the annual allocation of IAP money for Leicester, the case study area of primary concern in this book. Not only does it show the steady decline in funding in real terms since 1982/3, but the figures also contrast with the significant loss of other income to the City Council. On the Council's own figures more than £20 million was lost in reduced rate support grant between 1979/80 and 1986/87. More dramatically £122 million was lost from the Housing Investment Programme between 1979/80 and 1987/88.

Table 4 *Leicester's IAP allocation 1979/80 to 1987/8*

Year	Cash Allocation (£m)	Adjusted by GDP deflator (1980 = 100)
1979/80	2.78	3.33
1980/81	3.38	3.38
1981/82	4.16	3.73
1982/83	5.77	4.80
1983/84	6.50	5.15
1984/85	5.70	4.34
1985/86	5.83	4.19
1986/87	5.43	3.77
1987/88	5.43	3.70

Not only the size but the profile of expenditure within the programme has shifted in recent years. We shall examine this in some detail in Part Two. The most significant shifts within the urban programme as a whole reflect the government's growing concern that money should be spent on releasing enterprise, creating jobs and visibly salvaging the urban environment. Table 5 shows this shift clearly. Between 1979 and 1986 there was a marked movement of expenditure within the programme from social projects to environmental and economic projects, and from current to capital expenditure (that is, from people to things).

Equally significant has been the shift in both broad public expenditure and, more narrowly within the urban programme, towards policing the inner city. Urban policy initiatives have continued to be propelled by major disturbances. In April 1981 the Brixton riots were followed by further disturbances in

Table 5   *Shifts in the profile of urban programme expenditure 1979/80 to 1985/6ᵃ (%)*

	Economic	Environmental	Social	Current	Capital
1979/80	29	19	51	39	61
1985/86	34	23	43	34	66

Note: [a] Committee of Public Accounts (1986).

Southall, Moss Side in Manchester and Toxteth in Liverpool, which led to high profile action by the then Secretary of State, Michael Heseltine, particularly in Liverpool, and in Brixton following the publication of the Scarman Report. In 1985, major riots in Handsworth in Birmingham and in Tottenham and Brixton in London again produced flurries of activity and promises of action.

The result has been an increase in police service spending of 45 per cent in real terms between 1979 and 1986 (HC Hansard, 17 July 1987, WA col. 1425). Authorized police establishment strength in England and Wales rose from 84 758 in 1977 to 92 468 in 1985, requiring by 1986/7 expenditure of £3143 million (HM Chief Inspector of Constabulary, 1987). This pattern reflects political rather than police thinking, for as the Chief Inspector suggests, 'the root feelings of alienation and disillusionment expressed by militant sections of inner-city communities are largely beyond the influence of the police, and any strengthening of the police is unlikely to prevent riots from taking place' (p. 4).

Nonetheless the political thinking behind this pattern has been clearly evident, even within urban programme expenditure. Acutely conscious that, as the British Crime Survey showed, 'multi-racial areas and the poorest council estates show risks which are roughly three times above the average', the government allocated about 30 per cent of the resources available through the newly developed estates action programme in 1986/7 to 'provide increased security for residents on run-down council estates' (HC Hansard, 27 March 1987, WA col. 284). The almost biblical ideals of 1977 now found expression in video surveillance, 'defensible space', and strengthened management presence on decayed urban estates. As MP Winston Churchill argued, 'The regeneration of housing, business and jobs in the decaying and festering parts of our cities is urgent and overdue, but all efforts will be in vain unless those who live and work there can walk the streets in safety, and can feel secure in their homes' (HC Hansard, 17 July 1987, col. 1388).

There has thus been a marked shift in the pattern of expenditure targeted at urban problems, clearly reflecting the ways in which these problems have been defined. But how clearly targeted has this expenditure been? There are two complementary problems here. One is the presumption that urban deprivation is an essentially spatial problem, best tackled by area-based policies. The other is in locating the right areas, even assuming such policies are correct.

Who and where: the area approach to urban deprivation

The IAP is based upon the notion that resources should be channelled to particular cities whose inner areas exhibit signs of 'multiple urban deprivation'. As such, it is an 'area-based' policy, prioritizing deprived *areas* rather than deprived individuals or social groups.

The White Paper, *Policy for the Inner Cities* (1977) argued that

Many of the inner areas surrounding the centres of our cities suffer, in a marked way and to an unacceptable extent, from economic decline, physical decay and adverse social conditions. Inner area problems are a feature of many of our older towns. . . . Deprivation exists too in some pre- and post-war council estates, sometimes on the edge of the big cities. There is undoubtedly a need to tackle the problems of urban deprivation wherever they occur. But there must be a particular emphasis on the inner areas of some of the big cities because of the scale and intensity of their problems. (p. 2)

Setting the agenda for the IAP, the White Paper identified three main areas of concern: economic decline, physical conditions and social problems. It argued that poverty, unemployment and bad housing were concentrated in the inner cities, although some council estates outside the inner cities might also exhibit some of these problems. In particular, the White Paper argued that the 'inner areas of cities have a higher concentration of poor people', notably the elderly, the unemployed and ethnic minorities in addition to 'people with social needs requiring help and support' (p. 3). Finally, the White Paper argued that

there is a collective deprivation in some inner areas which affects all residents . . . This collective deprivation amounts to more than the sum of all individual disadvantages with which people have to contend. It is an important argument for tackling inner city deprivation on an area basis and for discriminating in favour of the inner areas in the working out of public policies and programmes. (p. 4)

The White Paper's arguments, as presented above, rest on three important assumptions:

1. There needs to be *discrimination* on an *area* basis.
2. The *inner* area of cities have a higher concentration of the poor, and thus should be the areas chosen for positive discrimination.
3. There is a '*collective deprivation*' such that the levels of welfare of deprived people are reduced even further by living near to other deprived people.

It is these basic assumptions which form the background to the area approach of the IAP and indeed to the other programmes of positive discrimination including Educational Priority Areas and the Community Development Projects. It is important to understand what these assumptions mean for the formulation and implementation of the IAP.

The first of the three assumptions is really concerned with the area approach itself. As with the UP before it, the IAP is 'an example *par excellence* of area-specific positive discrimination' (Edwards and Batley 1978. p. 13). The history of the area approach has been extensively documented (Edwards and Batley 1978; Eyles 1979) and rests on four main notions: poverty is a residual phenomenon found in small geographical areas ('pockets') in cities; that if the poor are still present in spite of a thorough-going welfare system then it must be due to some inadequacy on their part which requires selective state intervention; that there is a need to weight services and resources to particular areas so as to attempt to compensate 'for the handicaps imposed by the environment' (Plowden Report 1967, vol. 1); and finally, that local authority services require fuller coordination at the local level to meet the needs of the community.

It is for these reasons that the IAP attempts to 'tackle inner city deprivation on an area basis'. The areas chosen for special treatment are located in the inner cities. Importantly, however, it is left up to individual authorities to decide how to allocate their IAP resources within their inner city area.

As Brown and Madge (1982, p. 235) argue, effective policies to combat deprivation can be either selectively based or universal, and the justification for expending large proportions of available resources in a relatively few geographical areas depends on the concentrations of deprivation in these locations and on the nature of any association found between characteristics of people and characteristics of place. An interpretation of inner city deprivation and positive discrimination in this context, they argue, hangs on the answers to two empirical questions. Firstly, is the inner city really a special case in that it throws up unique patterns of problems? And secondly, are deprived areas and deprived people largely coincidental so that most people in the inner cities are similarly deprived and most deprived people are found in these locations? These two questions are central to the IAP.

The second assumption of the IAP is that most of the poor are concentrated in the inner cities, and that within the inner areas there are relatively small and compact areas wherein a high proportion of the population are deprived. While the White Paper acknowledged that deprivation could also exist on council estates on the edge of the cities, it nevertheless argued that most attention should be paid to the inner cities.

In examining the evidence concerning the relationship between deprived individuals and deprived areas however, Brown and Madge (1982) argue that it is 'very clear that not only are there enormous contrasts in circumstances among people living in the inner cities but also that many of the deprived live somewhere else entirely' (p. 237).

On the first point, the White Paper recognizes that the majority of inner city residents might have satisfactory homes and jobs, an observation corroborated empirically by Allnutt and Gelardi (1979). This does not mean that such persons are necessarily free from all kinds of deprivation; Allnut and Gelardi, for example, suggest they might still be affected by dereliction, vandalism and stigma. It does nevertheless demonstrate how misleading it can be to describe persons simply by where they live.

Ever where 'pockets' of deprivation can be shown to exist, evidence shows that there are still many people suffering from social deprivation who are located elsewhere. In the DoE's analysis of the 1971 census data, for example, Holtermann (1976) presented convincing evidence that individual aspects of deprivation were spread quite widely. For instance, in 1971 only 28 per cent of persons without an inside w.c. lived in the worst 5 per cent of Enumeration Districts (EDs) and only 61 per cent lived in the worst 15 per cent. Likewise the respective figures for overcrowding in the worst 5 and 15 per cent of EDs were 33 and 61 per cent. As Holtermann concluded, 'the degree of spatial concentration of individual aspects of deprivation is really quite low' (p. 44). In other words, the inner city did not have a monopoly on deprivation (Brown and Madge 1982, p. 238).

In a series of papers, Jarman (1983, 1984) produced 'underprivileged area scores' for all wards in England and Wales, using eight weighted variables. He found that among the 50 most 'underprivileged' 12 were in London, 10 in Birmingham, but hardly any were in the north-west and very few in cities like Manchester, Liverpool or Bradford.

Such conclusions are supported by Townsend (1979) in his survey of poverty in the UK:

Such findings confirm that an area strategy cannot be the cardinal means of dealing with poverty or 'under-privilege'. However we care to define economically or socially deprived areas, unless we include nearly half the areas in the country, there will be more poor persons or poor children living outside them than in them. There is a second conclusion. Within all or nearly all defined priority areas, there will be more persons who are not deprived than there are deprived. *Therefore discrimination based on ecology will miss out more of the poor or deprived than it will include.* (p. 56, our emphasis)

There is thus strong evidence from major national studies which questions the assumption that most of the poor and deprived are concentrated into relatively small geographical areas.

The third assumption of the White Paper is that there is collective urban deprivation in some areas of the inner city. This argument is an important part of the White Paper and several points need to be raised in relation to it.

Firstly, it is apparent that a link has traditionally been made between inner areas of cities and multiple deprivation. This is because these areas seem to display the most visible signs of social distress and physical neglect. However, as has been outlined above, research in the 1970s has demonstrated that deprivation is concentrated less in *areas* than within particular social *groups* (Brown and Madge 1982; Townsend 1979). That groups such as pensioners, families with young children, single parent families and the unemployed might themselves be found particularly on certain estates or in certain geographical areas is not disputed. The operation of the housing and labour markets means that the degree of mobility and choice of residence of such groups is typically more limited than for better-off groups (Sills, Taylor and Golding 1982). Nevertheless, it cannot simply be assumed that inner cities are a special case in that they throw up unique patterns of problems. Peripheral council estates have been shown, for example, to have significant proportions of deprived groups (English 1979; Holtermann 1976; McGregor 1979; Sills, Taylor and Golding 1982). Deprivation is a problem *in* inner cities (as it is in other areas), rather than a problem *of* inner cities.

Equally, deprivation is a problem *for* people, not *of* them. As Townsend (1987) points out

From a sociological perspective it is important to distinguish between the measurement of deprivation in different areas and the kind of people experiencing that deprivation, otherwise there is a danger of treating age, ethnicity and single parenthood as causes of the phenomenon under study. It is wrong in principle to treat being black or old and alone or a single parent as part of the definition of deprivation. Even if such people are deprived it is their deprivation and not their status which has to be measured. (p. 89)

The second point concerns the problems involved in actually trying to define what multiple deprivation is. The concept of *multiple* deprivation is based on the notion of people suffering simultaneously from different kinds of deprivation, for example, from both poor housing and a poor environment. This concept is extremely difficult to measure empirically for a number of reasons. First the census does not provide a complete picture of individual aspects of deprivation, let alone of multiple deprivation. Income data, for example, are not collected by the census and so 'proxy' measures such as car ownership have to be used despite their inadequacy. Other measures which could be argued as being important in assessing deprivation are also not adequately available, such as health levels, working conditions and security of employment, the level and quality of local public services, etc. (see Brown and Madge 1982; Holterman 1976). Secondly, even if one could measure all the factors contributing to deprivation one would still have to decide whether to combine them into a single measure of 'low welfare' or 'multiple deprivation'. There are technical problems involved here, such as how to weight individual indicators. Is, for example, poor housing more important than a poor environment? The main difficulty stems from our ignorance about the relative importance that deprived individuals themselves attach to the different dimensions of deprivation and the way the separate deprivations interact in their effect on welfare. In our own research (Sills, Tarpey and Golding 1981), for example, people were asked to rank their preferences for different areas of public expenditure, and it was found that individuals had a marked hierarchy of such preferences, with better housing and employment being especially important to them.

The most recent attempt at an official operationalization is the list of eight indicators of urban deprivation produced by the DoE in 1983, including unemployment, overcrowding, single pensioners, population change, and so on (DoE 1983). But no research into their interlinkage is available nor into whether other indicators would produce different ratings of areas.

From the census, all that can be done is to investigate the areas where there is simultaneously a high proportion of households or persons suffering one kind of deprivation *and* a high proportion suffering another kind. In such areas one *cannot* say whether it is the same individuals who have both kinds of deprivation. Thus, whilst it is technically possible to define 'multiply deprived' *areas*, it will not be the case that all who live in those areas will suffer from multiple, nor necessarily from individual aspects of deprivation. As Holtermann (1976) says: 'It must be repeated that one cannot say how many of the households in the Enumeration Districts with high levels of several deprivations are multiply deprived and, therefore, nothing can be said about the spatial distribution of mutliply deprived households' (p. 43).

Thus the defining of multiple deprivation, and the drawing of boundaries around 'areas of multiple deprivation' as defined by the census raise a number of problems. This is not to imply that multiple deprivation does not exist, but simply that no easy assumptions about its causes or nature, or about the location of multiply deprived households can be made. This was candidly admitted by a senior civil servant from the DoE on giving evidence to the Public Accounts Committee:

Our problem is that we can only measure deprivation by the statistics which are readily available and which are transferable between areas. Therefore, we do tend to lean on census data. We do not have such good measures in some sense for economic deprivation as for the proxies for social deprivation. It is partly simply a case that the statistical information is not available in a form that we can use. (Committee of Public Accounts 1985/6, para. 338).

The final point concerns the conceptual rather than the technical problems involved in defining multiple deprivation. The use of census data to measure personal characteristics is a widespread practice in exercises to 'map' deprivation. However, this whole method can be roundly criticized for its individualistic approach. Focusing on the characteristics of individuals or households fundamentally distorts conceptualization of the underlying causes of deprivation because it over-emphasizes individual circumstances and pathologies. This is particularly the case in studies of transmitted deprivation and 'cultures of poverty' (see Brown and Madge 1982).

A different approach would examine social, economic and environmental provision among groups or classes of people. In this approach, deprivation is seen in terms of the failure of particular groups to have access to a good labour market/house/ social environment/public transport system, etc. Those individuals or households suffering from multiple deprivation would themselves be most likely to have a poor labour market position.

To summarize, the White Paper, and indeed the IAP itself, is based on a number of assumptions about the nature of 'urban' problems which have been questioned by major national studies of the nature and distribution of deprivation in society. The IAP is based fundamentally on the notion of positive discrimination. However, such positive action can take a number of forms not all of which are complementary. To discriminate in favour of deprived groups is *not* necessarily compatible with a policy of discriminating in favour of deprived areas and vice versa.

It is common in studies of deprivation to fall into the ecological trap of assuming that the majority if not all individuals in a sub-area conform to the pattern of characteristics derived from aggregate data, but there is also the problem of assuming that those who suffer from individual aspects or from multiple deprivation are more spatially concentrated than is actually the case. These problems means that area-based policies will have difficulty in targeting services and facilities to particular deprived groups.

In recent years targeting has thus become increasingly diffuse. By 1987/8 no fewer than 57 authorities were preparing IAPs, compared with 24 in 1979/80. The political implications are extensive. No fewer than 152 constituencies in England (nearly 30 per cent of the total) contain areas receiving urban programme and inner city initiative support (HC Hansard, 20 February 1987, WA col. 851–4). We examine the distribution of assisted priority zones in Leicester's IAP in Chapters 4 and 5.

Conclusion

In this chapter we have examined the political, ideological and economic bases of policies aimed at tackling urban deprivation, particularly the IAP. As we have seen, shifts in public expenditure have penalized severely just those populations and areas singled out for assistance through inner city initiatives. The scale of these penalties tends to dwarf resources available in the more specific programmes. However, the definition of the problem is seen to focus, firstly, on the problems of the people living in inner city areas and, secondly, or the local government activities in those areas.

The first of these emphases suggests small targeted financial packages can regenerate the energies and enterprise of inner city residents, creating a new harmony and communal spirit. These packages are necessarily cheap because fiscal pressures constrain the available resources. But they are high profile and, we suggest, primarily aimed at symbolic reassurance of potentially troublesome urban populations. The second emphasis justifies the vast reduction in central government funding of local authorities to tackle the problem, as the 1986 Green Paper put it, that 'adult members of ratepayer's families may have even less appreciation of the cost of local services' (Cmnd 9714, *Paying for Local Government*, 1986, p. 6). The burden is to be shifted, as we discuss in the conclusion to this book, to local ratepayers, and hopes for urban renewal are to be based on the private sector. In the Prime Minister's view, 'One of the difficulties about inner cities is that some councils are positively hostile to the private sector, which could solve their problems' (HC Hansard, 2 July 1987, col. 622).

If resources are reduced, they are, as we have seen, spread thinly as an increasing proportion of the population is drawn into the definition of areas needing assistance. These definitions, based in part on response to urban disorder, in part on unsatisfactory statistical bases, become increasingly removed from the root material deprivations of the growing mass of urban poor in late twentieth-century Britain.

In the remaining chapters, we take a close look at the attempt to implement those changing policies at local level by examining in detail the political, social and economic dimensions of the IAP in one city.

Part Two

4 A programme without a policy

Introduction

In the following three chapters we examine the IAP in detail through analysing its political, economic and social dynamics in one city, Leicester. An East Midland city of some 280 000 people, it was formerly a very prosperous manufacturing area specializing in hosiery and knitwear, footwear and engineering. By the latter half of the 1970s, however, the city was experiencing the effects of a rapid declining industrial base and record levels of unemployment. This rising unemployment, together with inadequate housing and a poor environment in its inner city areas made Leicester a prime candidate for the new IAP resources. In addition, the city's ethnic minority population had grown significantly in the 1970s, notably with the settling of East African Asians expelled from Idi Amin's Uganda, resulting in some 24 per cent of city residents being from ethnic minorities by the early 1980s.

Leicester was declared a programme authority in 1978, one of the first fifteen of such authorities eligible for IAP funds. In many respects, Leicester is an exemplary IAP authority. It has always taken the IAP and the resources it brings with it very seriously. The following chapters highlight the organizational and procedural changes instigated by Leicester City Council in response to the IAP. New groups of officers and members were set up to discuss the social, environmental and economic problems and needs of the city and its residents, and to assess new projects to be set up using IAP funds in response to these issues. The IAP brought not only changes within Leicester City Council, however, but from the start gave a new impetus and focus to the voluntary sector. Leicester took the decision early on to involve voluntary projects as much as possible in the IAP, and the developing statutory–

voluntary relationship has been a major feature of the programme in the city. Leicester has used its IAP resources to develop new initiatives in all three aspects of the programme: under the 'social' element it has funded a huge variety of projects, particularly from the voluntary sector; the 'environmental' resources have been largely used to fund highly visible improvements to the physical fabric of the inner city; and the economic aspect of the programme has also become increasingly important, not least because of DoE guidelines that more of the IAP funds should be spent on economic projects. The diversity and impact of this activity is examined in the following chapters.

Given the limited funds of a district authority like Leicester City Council, particularly in a period of continued controls on council expenditure, Leicester has accorded considerable importance to the IAP. The programme has been important not only because of the extra resources it provides, although these are not inconsiderable (a total of £5.4 million annually by 1987) but also the IAP looked particularly attractive because its funds are largely uncommitted and thus they appeared to afford councillors a high degree of flexibility in determining how they are spent, unusual within the local government financial framework. In short, the IAP seemed to afford councillors a degree of political largesse practically no other source of expenditure could allow, making it at once both a politically attractive and powerful mechanism. The degree to which the IAP fulfilled this ambition is examined in detail in subsequent chapters.

Finally, it is necessary here to briefly outline the geographical basis on which Leicester's IAP was established. Once declared a programme authority, the city council had very rapidly to define those areas of the city within which it could target its IAP resources. On the basis of census data, Leicester took the decision to define seven distinct 'priority zones'. Four of these were classic 'inner city' districts of largely private or mixed housing, but three were outer area council estates which exhibited poverty and deprivation on a scale similar to (and in some cases worse than) the inner city districts. These seven zones, then, in 1979 formed the basis for the new and exciting IAP in Leicester.

The IAP: structure and process

The IAP is concerned with both means and ends. It is as interested in how a policy is implemented as in the goals to be achieved. In this chapter we discuss the interrelationship between means and ends in the IAP, examining both the objectives of the IAP and the mechanisms by which these were to be secured, focusing in particular on the extent to which the structures and processes of the IAP supported or frustrated its aims. We will be examining three main issues: the concept of partnership in the IAP; the IAP planning process; and finally the issue of monitoring the results from the IAP process.

Partnership in the IAP

In its new initiative towards the inner city, the government attached great importance to the *means* by which its policies were to be achieved, with the means being as important as the ends. The key concept here was the notion of a partnership for the inner city whereby the agencies of central and local government would join forces with the private sector and the communities that lived in the inner city, working together to tackle the problems of urban deprivation. The act of working together in partnership was seen to have three main advantages:

1. *Cooperation between agencies.* The White Paper stressed the advantages of a combined approach by government agencies:

   The urban studies of recent years have shown that urban problems cannot be tackled effectively on a piecemeal basis. The problems interlock: education, for example, is affected by social conditions which in turn are affected by housing and by employment. The best results are likely to be achieved through a unified approach in which the different activities and services of government are brought together. Concerted action should have a greater impact. (House of Commons 1977, para. 59)

   Thus partnership was seen to secure the cooperation necessary for a unified approach that would be more effective.
2. *Extra resources.* A second major advantage of partnership was that the government could claim that the resources to be devoted to this massive task were far in excess of the grant-

aided inner city programme. The advantage of a partnership was that it could call on resources from both the public sector, through the redirection of main programme expenditure and an enhanced rate support grant allocation, and resources from the private investment as well.

3. *Self-help*.   The importance of involving local residents in tackling the problems of the inner city is a common feature of poverty programmes. For the White Paper this was seen to be 'both a necessary means of regenerating the inner areas and an end in its own right' (para. 34). The advantages of this extended partnership were twofold: firstly, that public authorities could 'draw on the ideas of local residents, to discover their priorities and enable them to play a practical part in reviving their areas' (para. 34) and secondly, that 'some things will be better done, or done more satisfactorily, if they are undertaken by voluntary groups and bodies' (para. 35). Partly this extension of partnership was intended to tap the enthusiasm and ideas of local people and partly as an encouragement to participation, which was seen as an antidote to apathy.

Partnership as a means of securing a revival of the inner city encounters a number of problems. Do common goals exist to provide a basis for partnership or is the conflict that exists between agencies and interests one of the principal causes of inner city decay? If there are no common policy objectives then it follows that there will be little cooperation between agencies and few, if any, additional resources. As part of an exercise in symbolic reassurance the concept of partnership succeeded in constructing the necessary referential context for the inner city. However, as a means to securing a revival of the inner city, its failure to take account of political realities made it a non-starter.

The IAP planning process

If partnership was to be the means of securing a revival of the inner city, the method of securing the partnership was to be through the participation of the partners in the preparation of a joint IAP Submission Document. This document was to incorporate a description of the problems of the inner city, a list of objectives outlining appropriate action to be taken, a statement of how the main programme activities of the principal partners affected the inner city, and a programme of projects which both complemented main programme activity and for which grant aid was requested. The process of preparing this submission document, determining the policies and the projects to be included has been central to the IAP. Indeed it is debatable whether much of any significance has been stimulated by the IAP outside of this process. It is vital, therefore, to examine the IAP planning process to see how the structures and processes set up to prepare the annual IAP Submission Documents have supported or frustrated the aims of the IAP.

In both its structure and processes the IAP conformed with the current wisdom of the day that stressed the advantages of funding local authority activity through the mechanism of special programmes and was similar in style to both the Housing Investment Programme (HIP) and the Transport Policies and Programmes (TPP) that preceded it. Collectively these programmes have been referred to as Policy Planning Systems (PPS).

A Policy Planning System is perhaps most usefully seen as an instrument for making explicit, formalising and regulating the relations between objectives, policies and finance, in a particular policy sector. It is invariably premised upon some version of the rational planning model of policy-making, and embodies at least a medium-term planning horizon together with built-in review mechanisms. (Leach and Stewart 1983, p. 23)

Leach and Stewart identify the principal features of a PPS, which are seen to apply to the IAP: a comprehensive approach, which emphasizes the need to involve all related agencies in an integrated response; a rationality based process, which is based on a rational model of policy-making; future orientation of policy, emphasizing the need for a long-term commitment; and a medium-term rolling programme; local autonomy, stressing the need for local flexibility in assessing needs, determining priorities and prescribing action; and finally financial control, whereby central government exercises influence both on the overall level of resource allocation and on what the allocation can be spent through the use of specific grants.

The IAP can be seen as a poverty programme designed in the format of a PPS. The problem that the IAP encountered was that, lacking any clear objectives, the policy element in the process was rapidly relegated as the complexities of programming took precedence. Hence the IAP became a programme without a policy. In place of a locally determined, local coordinated comprehensive attack on the problems of urban deprivation, the IAP has degenerated into an annual resource allocation exercise which is severely constrained by rules devised in Whitehall. How and why this has happened and its implications, both specifically for the preparation of the annual IAP and also for inner city policy in general, are examined below.

Following the PPS model outlined above, the White Paper, in both its language and its assumptions, proposed that partnership and programme authorities should adopt the rational model of policy-making when constructing their IAPs. The rational model sees policy-making as a cyclical process involving six related stages; an identification of problems and the formulation of objectives to tackle them, the generation and examination of alternative courses of action, followed by the implementation of preferred option and the monitoring of progress.

Using the logic of the rational model, local authorities were invited to prepare their IAPs. We shall examine each stage in this process to see how attempts in Leicester to introduce a framework of rationality to the IAP have been undermined, both by conceptual weaknesses in the original strategy and by the practical problems that have emerged in attempting to make it work.

Stage 1: Identifying the problem

The first stage in the rational model is to identify the problem to be addressed. This was to be a major weakness of the IAP. At the conceptual level there was little understanding of what the 'inner city problem' was, and at the practical level, little time to consider, define or measure it.

When the Secretary of State announced the list of partnership and programme authorities to receive an enhanced urban aid allocation these authorities had less than a year to prepare their first IAPs. The clear impression given by both ministers and civil servants was of the paramount need to get something done in line with the government's new commitment to the inner cities. Thus none of the 'partners' had any but the vaguest of notions as to what was required and requests for further clarification from the

DoE were met by reminders about the experimental nature of the IAP and the need for locally determined programmes. Indeed, local authorities were left with the understanding that the first year of the IAP was essentially one of trial and error and that many of the problems would be rectified in subsequent years. The key word for the first year was *action*.

This in practice was to prove a major stumbling block to the attempt to introduce a rational approach to the IAP. When local authorities were confronted by the need to establish both a new inter-corporate structure for preparing the IAP and a system for generating and selecting bids (including bids from the voluntary sector) they had little time to consider exactly where or what the 'inner city problem' was.

The lack of a strong theoretical justification for the IAP can be seen in the system created for the distribution of IAP resources. The positive discrimination of the IAP worked at two levels, both between and within cities. IAP resources were made available in 22 authorities, being 7 partnership authorities and 15 programme authorities. In the designation of IAP authorities, it is difficult to see any precise criteria at work. Early in 1977, the DoE let it be known that something was in the air and invited local authorities to submit details of inner city areas and the problems therein. There then followed a period of 'horse trading', when some got in and others were rejected. Whatever assessment criteria were used, it was not that of urban deprivation. This is made clear in the White Paper's insistence that positive discrimination should occur *within* cities, drawing a distinction between urban deprivation (a general condition found in many urban areas) and the needs of the inner city, which will receive priority:

Inner area problems are a feature of many of our older towns but they are at their most serious in the major cities. In small cities and older industrial areas there are substantial areas of decay, bad housing, poor employment and social problems. Deprivation exists too in some pre- and post-war council estates, sometimes on the edge of the big cities. There is undoubtedly a need to tackle the problems of urban deprivation wherever they occur. But there must be a particular emphasis on the inner areas of some of the big cities because of the scale and intensity of their problems and the rapidity of run-down in population and employment. (para. 6)

The necessity for the IAP to be directed specifically at the ghetto is shown by the further insistence by the DoE that IAP resources are directed to the inner city parts of the designated authorities, *regardless* of whether they consider the problems to be the most severe in those areas or capable of treatment on an area basis. Certainly, given the wealth of evidence that exists disputing the existence of concentrations of deprivation at either a national or local level, combined with the DoE's insistence on a marked degree of geographical bias in the allocation of resources, explanations for this policy must be sought elsewhere. The difference between poverty in general and poverty in the ghetto is that the latter is a political priority because of its relationship with public order.

Local authorities welcomed the additional resources made available to them through the IAP, but, given the pronounced lack of direction from central government in this initial stage of planning process, it is hardly surprising that local authorities restricted themselves to a rapid review of existing data sources to determine which areas would benefit. Planning departments were called on to produce a quick reworking of the 1971 census data, looking for spatial concentrations of anything that might resemble deprivation, whilst other departments looked at what data they held that might similarly reveal incidences of this new phenomenon. Local authorities were required to produce a map demonstrating the existence of an inner city problem that would justify their status as an inner city authority.

In Leicester, the justification of IAP status was on the basis of analysis of twenty variables drawn from the 1971 census data. This analysis produced the geographical framework which guided the distribution of resources through Leicester's IAP so it warrants closer examination (Sills, Taylor and Golding 1983a). Due to the government's insistence on instant action, Leicester's IAP, like those in all other authorities, was prepared at rapid speed and heavy reliance was placed on census data. However, the approach adopted in Leicester had three main weaknesses. The variables selected were chosen on the basis of their ready availability rather than from any clear analysis of what 'urban deprivation' might be. As we have seen, the census provides information which is strongly weighted towards housing standards and tenure, and thus 'housing factors' figured predominantly in the list of indicators used to select the priority zones. However, the main reason that housing factors were so emphasized in Leicester's definition of its inner area was because it used precisely the same statistical

analysis which had been previously undertaken to select the
housing renewal strategy zones. Whilst the census provides the
data necessary to select areas with deficient housing conditions, it
cannot be simply assumed that such areas are also areas of multiple
deprivation.

A second weakness is that the indicators used in the definition
of Leicester's priority zones not only heavily emphasized 'housing
factors' in general (no less than ten of the twenty indicators used
in the statistical (factor) analysis related directly to housing
conditions and tenure), but also emphasized particular *types* of
housing factors. Although the DoE itself stressed the importance
of housing in its initial guidelines for the drawing up of the IAP,
the variables chosen for inclusion in the factor analysis were ones
which *assumed* the importance of private sector housing conditions
and which underestimated the importance of public sector housing
conditions. This was, of course, a reflection of the factor analysis's
former role in defining renewal strategy zones.

A third problem was that the census variables failed to provide
any conceptual definition of inner city problems and were, by
1978, seriously out of date.

For this first programme, the Inner Area of Leicester has been defined
largely on the basis of the 1971 Census . . . It must be acknowledged
that such an analysis is very limited in terms of the total amount of 'stress'
which is identified. It does not include other measures such as crime,
poverty, harassment, etc., which are perhaps more germane to a consideration of stress in the Inner Area. Equally the Census data on which the
analysis is based is now some 7 years old . . . Thus the interpretation of
the factors must be carried out with caution, and the City Council will
keep the definition of the Inner Area under constant review. (Leicester
City Council 1978, p. 2)

Despite this commitment to review, the importance of this initial
analysis in determining the geographical boundaries for Leicester's
IAP has been increasingly apparent. Over the years the establishment of structured processes designed to support the IAP, such
as area review teams of officers established in each of the seven
priority zones, mitigated against any fundamental change in the
designated areas.

The Inner Area Studies of Lambeth, Liverpool and Birmingham, commissioned by the DoE, stressed the primary importance of economic factors underlying the structural interpretation

of poverty put forward by the CDPs. Unwilling, or unable, to cope with the implications of a radical theory of the causes of poverty, but with no credible alternative to put in its place, the government ducked the issue in *Policy for the Inner City* by providing neither a theory of deprivation nor a clear statement as to how it should be tackled. In place of an analysis of the issue the government put forward its 'comprehensive approach' to the inner cities. In essence the inner city problem was seen as the sum of the problems found in the inner city! Thus the economic, environmental and social problems of the inner city were described and the virtues of a combined attack by all agencies extolled but there was no explanation given as to fundamental causes or how these could be best controlled. It is obvious that if the first stage of a planning process is inadequate or incomplete, that of defining the basic problem to be addressed, this has major implications for the effectiveness of the stages that follow.

Stage 2: Setting objectives

Again both conceptual and practical difficulties were experienced at this stage. At the conceptual level a great deal has been written about the problems of goal-setting in the public sector. Do public organizations have clear objectives and, if they do, can they be stated in a way that enables performance to be reviewed? Is the political process, with its emphasis on short-term flexibility, at odds with a planning process that attempts to define policy objectives over a much longer term horizon? Clearly any attempt by local authorities to use the rational planning model when formulating inner city strategies was going to encounter difficulties. In part this explains the vague nature of the objectives that frequently feature in IAP documents, such as 'to improve the environment' or 'to revive the economy'. This lack of precision hampered the IAP both in the short term, making it difficult to select IAP bids or to redirect main programmes in a way that conformed to the programme's strategy. Equally, in the long term, there was no yardstick by which to assess the effectiveness of IAP policy as a whole.

In addition to the conceptual problems surrounding goal setting, there was the practical difficulty of deciding whose objectives the IAP was to represent. *Policy for the Inner Cities* attempted to bring together in partnership all the groups interested in reviving the inner city. The implicit assumption was that these groups shared common interests, ignoring the fact that many of the problems in the inner city were the result of conflicting interests. It is difficult to see how the notion of an IAP built on partnership and common objectives can be reconciled with the political realities of competing claims on resources. These difficulties and the attempts to reconcile them are illustrated in the case of Leicester's IAP.

The approach adopted by Leicester City Council reflected a genuine commitment to the concept of partnership reinforced by a strong sense of pragmatism about how this could be achieved. With reorganization in 1974 Leicester City Council lost its responsibility for both education and social services to the county council, a fact still uppermost in its mind in 1977, when the two authorities were asked to prepare a joint IAP. Obviously for the city council the opportunity was offered either to use the IAP to exert influence over county council services, or to make political capital out of the county's lack of cooperation. At this time, Peter Shore was making noises about the possibility of 'organic change', giving certain strategic functions back to districts in major urban areas.

For its part the county council was extremely wary of this wooden horse of partnership but was reluctant to forego the opportunity of grant aid. Thus, while certain senior members and officers in both councils remained committed to the principles of IAP, the practical problem of developing a structure that could accommodate the various interests remained. The solution was to base the IAP around six key issues, which reflected the professional interests of six main departments of both councils. Each key issue was examined by a group of officers, four groups chaired by officers from the city council and two by officers from the county.

In practice each key issue working group was autonomous, with the chairman of each being in a position of professional authority. Each group reported back to a steering group of chief officers where again the chairmen were in a position to enforce their own preferences should a dispute develop, which it rarely did. Thus the city council had succeeded in drawing the county council into its partnership whilst the county council could still enforce its own policies and preferences in its own service areas. However, this professional stranglehold on Leicester's IAP was at the expense of either voluntary sector or political parties. Tensions came to a head in 1982 when councillors chose to prepare their own programme, making their own selection of projects, mainly from the voluntary sector.

Stage 3: Generating alternatives

Having identified the problems to be tackled, Stage 3 in the planning cycle generates a range of alternative actions that can be evaluated against the programme's objectives. In the IAP alternatives are generated through a bidding process whereby statutory agencies and voluntary groups can submit proposals for projects for which IAP funding is requested.

In attempting to operate the IAP in this way local authorities encountered three main problems.

Firstly, at a practical level it is debatable to what extent inner city groups have been able to respond to partnership through bidding for resources to the IAP. The invitation to partnership presumes a knowledge of the IAP and the opportunities it presents, and the confidence and ability to submit a project and bargain with public agencies. Our research in Leicester found that the level of understanding of the IAP process amongst community groups was low and that there was resentment expressed at the complexity of the IAP rules and bid forms, which were interpreted by many as deliberate barriers to partnership.

This research in Leicester suggested how difficult it has been for the city council to get projects from grass roots community groups which the council was committed to supporting. Indeed the vast majority of the bids received from such groups were, on close examination, prepared by council officers – an unexpected partnership of 'them' and 'us'. Whilst the assistance was necessary, it was open to abuse, and in a number of cases voluntary sector bids were being used as a smokescreen for departmental activities. By contrast, voluntary groups with a strong middle-class professional input are much better placed to take advantage of the IAP and to maintain a measure of independence from their local authority partners. We examine this problem further in Chapter 6.

Secondly, in addition to questioning whether the bidding process can key into and stimulate self-help and community effort amongst inner city residents, it is also questionable to what extent

IAP bids can be seen to reflect needs within the community. This raises fundamental issues for the government's inner city strategy. A major element in the IAP is the funding of special projects. These projects are selected from a range of bids submitted. An assumption underlying this model is that there is a strong relationship between bids made to the IAP and the needs of the communities that submit them. Again our research in Leicester suggests that the relationship between bids and needs is more complex. A central problem is that as the residents of some areas are more willing and able to submit IAP bids than others, can bids for the IAP reflect anything other than the ability to submit IAP bids? Obviously, whilst bids are subject to both professional and political scrutiny, nonetheless only those bids submitted to the IAP can be included in the final programme. Can an IAP strategy be left dependent on the bids it receives? Here there is the problem of reconciling the strategy and priorities of the local authority with the initiative and ideas of various groups in the inner city. In practice, it has proved difficult to permit sufficient room for local initiative if the strategy is too tightly defined, whilst an alternative approach that permits a maximum degree of freedom to groups in submitting bids run into the danger of having no recognizable strategy at all and simply reproducing and enhancing existing inequalities of service provision between areas.

A third problem with the bidding process is that although bids generate alternatives it does not follow that these alternatives represent the best way of tackling the problem to hand. This problem can be seen in the use made of the IAP to support hostel accommodation in Leicester (see Sills, Taylor and Golding 1982). The IAP has been used in Leicester to support the provision of hostel accommodation for the single homeless. Given the problems of homelessness and the availability of IAP resources hostel provision seemed an obvious answer. However, on further examination of the housing needs of many hostel residents, it was found that they were rarely the 'special needs' assumed by the Housing Department, but were capable of being met through main programme housing provision. Thus the IAP had been used, in effect, to marginalize a problem that should have been tackled through the council's own allocation policy.

Stage 4: Evaluating alternatives

When bids are received the fourth stage in the IAP cycle is to assess their relative merits and assemble an IAP. Given the problems identified in the preceding three stages, this was always going to present problems. If the conception of deprivation was a generous one and the objectives employed similarly wide ranging, then the evaluation of bids occurs in a strategic vacuum, with each being assessed 'on its merits'. In practice, a group of senior members and/or officers sit down with a large pile of bids and choose which ones will be included in the IAP on the basis of the extent to which the bid's objectives, costs and the group submitting the application meet with the professional and political preferences of the council. Over the years, the strategic element of the IAP has been jettisoned as councils have been forced to concentrate on the programming aspects entailed in preparing the annual IAP.

There are two main factors that have, in effect, reduced the IAP to an annual resource allocation exercise: firstly, those developments common to programming as a whole, and secondly, those features specific to the IAP.

As we have outlined at the start of this chapter, programming is a particular type of policy vehicle designed to link strategy and resources in areas in which central and local government have a joint concern. However, as Leach and Stewart (1983) have shown, the use of programming has changed over the years. They detect a

movement from an emphasis on strategy to an emphasis on programmes; from a concern with the rationality of the process to concern with the content of the programmes; from a broad policy focus to a (relatively) narrow one; from an attempt at medium-term resource planning to an overriding concern with next year's programme and with financial control aspects thereof; from an emphasis on joint planning to a form of bidding system; and finally from an explicit concern with local knowledge/ autonomy to an implicit central dominance. (Leach and Stewart 1983, p. 267)

In addition to the general problems associated with PPSs, however, there are two specific problems which have reduced the strategic element in the IAP.

Firstly, there is no tolerance or carry forward of expenditure from one financial year to the next permitted in the IAP. It is normal in local authority accounting to permit resources that have not been spent in one financial year to be carried forward to the next. However, expenditure, especially of an experimental nature, is notoriously difficult to control to the fine level required by the DoE. Inevitably, projects start late and their expenditure 'slips' into the following year, making it the first call on expenditure in the next year's programme. This lack of certainty concerning resource availability undermines strategic planning, with local authorities having to spend a great deal of time in estimating what level of resources they may have available to allocate through the IAP. Local authorities thus have to make a number of calculations when preparing an IAP. How much expenditure will slip over from the current year's IAP and then, given the need to try to spend a full 100 per cent of their allocation, how much does their programme have to be over-bid to compensate for slippage?

A second factor reducing the strategic element in the IAP are government guidelines on the IAP. These insist that local authorities, when preparing their IAP, have regard to the balance of expenditure both between topics (economic, environmental or social projects) and between types of expenditure (capital or revenue).

What do these programming problems mean to a local authority when it attempts to prepare an IAP? In particular, how do the constraints of preparing affect local autonomy and strategic choice? What influence do the rules that govern the IAP have on local decision-making? We examined the difficulties encountered by Leicester City Council in its attempts to prepare its 1983/4 IAP.

At the start of the process an estimation had to be made of the level of resources that would be available that year. This entailed making informed assumptions about a number of issues (Table 6). Firstly, an estimate was made of the total value of the 1983/4 IAP (Stage 1) from which can be deducted an estimate of existing commitments (Stage 2), which form the first call on IAP resources. To this new figure is added in an estimation for likely under-spending from the 1983/4 IAP (Stage 3). Thus, if slippage is estimated at 25 per cent then an IAP has to be 25 per cent larger to ensure a full take-up of allocation. Finally, in Stage 4 the estimated amount of new money for projects is divided with regard to the government's guidelines regarding both topics and capital–revenue split. In such a calculation a deviation in any one of the assumptions can have major implications for the final outcome. For example, with only an estimated £0.3 million available for revenue expenditure could the city council justify inviting bids from the voluntary sector at all? The programming constraints were suggesting that the city council should attempt to prepare an IAP that had a capital–revenue split of £2.3 to £0.3 million that gave a distribution of resources across the main expenditure

Table 6   *Forecast of likely IAP resources for 1983/4 (£m)*

Stage 1   Estimate 1983/4 allocation
Assumption – City council gets same allocation as
1982/3 (in real terms)   Estimate 4.8

Stage 2   Deduct commitments   −3.5

Assumptions – 10% inflation Nov. 1980–Nov. 1981   1.4
– Slippage in equals slippage out
– All projects financed under section
137 Act proceed

Stage 3   Overbid

Assumption – Slippage will be 25% of estimated   2.6 (for new
allocation   projects)

Stage 4   Allocate new money

1. Between topics
Assumptions – The programme should represent a
balance between DoE advice (40/
20/30) and 1982/3 IAP (33/26/41)

Economic	*Environment*	*Social*
37%	26%	37%
1.8	0.3	0.5

2. Between capital and revenue

	Capital	*Revenue*
Total programme	3.8	2.2
Commitments	1.5	1.9
New money	2.3	0.3

NB: All prices at November 1981 price base

heads of £1.8 million (economic), £0.3 million (environment) and £0.5 million (social).

This was the situation facing Leicester City Council as it attempted to prepare its IAP in 1982. Clearly it is not easy to understand and it is unlikely whether more than a few chief officers and councillors were fully aware of the many complexities involved in the calculations. What we see here is the programming element of the IAP dominating over policy considerations.

Clearly this situation has moved a considerable distance away from the intentions of *Policy for the Inner Cities* which saw local authorities as being the 'natural agencies to tackle inner area problems' (para. 31). There is a clear absence of any strategic element to the IAP if local authorities are primarily engaged in an annual resource allocation exercise, attempting to design a programme in accordance with the government's guidelines. Within the constraints there is very little room for locally determined policies. Leicester City Council has consistently argued, for example, that the problems that exist in Leicester can be dealt with more effectively through the IAP by projects of a 'social' nature, involving revenue expenditure, but running counter to the government's guidelines. Finally, the planning horizon for the IAP has been reduced to the shortest of short terms. With the uncertainties surrounding local authority finance in general and the future of the IAP in particular it is now impossible to prepare a three-year rolling programme for the IAP that represents anything more than a paper commitment.

The problems associated with rate-capping, encountered in 1985, made the situation even more bizarre, with projects that were included in the IAP and approved by the DoE, yet having no clear starting date due to lack of local authority resources. In reality, the IAP is now merely an annual allocation exercise for a grant-aided programme of projects. Any strategic element it may have had has vanished under an array of rules and regulations. A programme designed to release the energies and enterprise of local communities could hardly have a wider gulf between its intentions and the means to realize them.

Stage 5: Implementation

One of the advantages of a PPS is its ability to bring policy decisions together with the resources to implement them. So it is surprising that the IAP has experienced major problems in its implementation.

Each partnership or programme authority must submit its IAP to the DoE. The DoE considers which projects to approve and the overall level of resources to be allocated to each authority. The delay and uncertainties involved cause problems for implementation. Without a knowledge of either the total amount of grant aid approved or of the individual projects, or the way in which this money can be spent, local authorities are naturally cautious of undertaking preparatory work before official notification is received from the DoE. As this official approval can come as late as July it can cause problems for a programme that is meant to have commenced in April! Thus the programme year is in effect squeezed at both ends: at the beginning, with late approval by the DoE, and at the end, with no allowance available to carry forward finance into the subsequent year.

The financial constraints operating on the IAP are unusually tight when compared to those that govern local authority finance in general. The problem of implementing the IAP is compounded, however, by its emphasis on experimentation. IAP projects are not meant to be mere extensions of local authority main programme activities. Many involve either new areas of operation for local government, such as law centres or economic projects, or new ways of operating, as in partnership with voluntary groups. Whilst this emphasis on innovation is central to the IAP, it can, by necessity, be at odds with the demands for speedy and efficient implementation. Bureaucracies are good at administration but are less good at creating new ways of working.

The final problem that the IAP presents for implementation is the speculative nature of many of its projects. A bid to the IAP is a bid for resources. A voluntary group or a statutory department makes a bid to the IAP in one year to implement a project in the next. If the bid is approved its sponsors have to ensure its implementation. This entails trying to get both the right staff and a suitable building in the right area. For a number of projects the gap between bidding for resources and implementing a scheme proves unbridgeable, and the venture never gets off the ground. There is enormous tension between the innovative intentions of the IAP and its restrictive mechanisms, which has yet to be resolved. The IAP is intended to provide projects that are different from the mainstream services of local government, but the funding arrangements which have been established to support the IAP often frustrate this objective.

Stage 6: Monitoring and review

The final stage in the planning cycle is the monitoring of activities and reviewing their contribution to the original objectives that guided the programme's formulation. As the IAP was seen to be a learning programme, this stage is considered to be crucial to the success of the entire inner city initiative.

Experimentation and review provide the rationale for tackling urban deprivation through a programme of special projects and are used also to explain the financial arrangements involved. These two issues will be examined in turn.

It was argued in the White Paper that there is a need for special programmes because there is a need to experiment with new ideas and new approaches. The major programmes of central and local government it is argued, have failed to eliminate poverty because they have either lacked selectivity, failing to help the really poor, or have adopted either the wrong methods of service delivery or the wrong priorities. As a result, the most efficient way of tackling poverty is not merely to provide 'more of the same' but to search out new approaches which can inform and improve current practice. In line with this commitment to experimentation, an integral part of the IAP was its commitment to monitoring and research: 'The results of the programmes will need to be assessed to see that they are achieving the results desired, and so that lessons can be learnt (para. 81).

Not only was the IAP intended to produce innovative projects it was also meant to develop new organizational forms and political structures: 'The powers and finances of central and local government will need to be used in a unified and coherent way. New forms of organization and new methods' (para. 70).

In both partnership and programme authorities new committees were created to administer the IAP, drawing their membership from outside the local authority and, in some cases, including representatives from the voluntary sector.

The funding arrangements for special programmes also owe much to their experimental nature. Firstly, it explains the rationale for joint funding, with, in the case of the IAP, central government providing 75 per cent of the finance and local government the remaining 25 per cent. It is argued that as local authorities are being asked to undertake experimental projects that lie outside their normal range of activities these experiments should be, in part, financed by central government. Secondly, because these *are* experiments, the period of joint funding is limited to four years for voluntary projects and three for statutory schemes. By the end of this period the experiment will have been completed and, if successful, the project can be taken into an authority's main programme activity without the support of central government finance.

The commitment to an innovative programme has also been used as a justification for the small budget allocated to the IAP. As an experimental programme the IAP is a commitment to future action. Thus the emphasis on experimentation is a way of reconciling the seriousness of the government's stated objective of tackling the problems of poverty with the plainly inadequate resources allocated to the task. This credibility gap between commitment and resources is bridged by the overtures to experimentation. Whilst the programme is small, its implications are massive. What is needed above all is new ideas. Once the way has been found, then the resources will follow. Seen in this light innovation takes on a central role in the IAP, both in terms of strategy and credibility.

If the IAP is to be used as an experimental programme then clearly the monitoring and review stage is of special importance. Local authorities were invited to prepare IAPs in which a programme of projects had been selected to meet the identifiable needs of their inner city areas. These projects were to be monitored and their results fed back into the local authority's main programmes and also passed on to central government. Through the process of identifying local needs and experimenting with a variety of alternative responses, local authorities were to improve their public learning, both in terms of problem recognition and adaptive capacity.

Efforts to use the IAP as a vehicle for experimentation have met with difficulties, due to both lack of resources and as the result of government guidelines. Resource constraints within the public sector have, in effect, put a brake on experimentation. The IAP is most active in the areas in which public expenditure cuts have been most severe (housing, social services). At a time when the attention of councillors and chief officers is focused firmly on protecting basic standards in main programme activities, it is understandable that many do not have the inclination, or the resources, for experimentation.

Whilst a classical economic model would see 'necessity as the mother of invention', this is to ignore the strong influence of departmental inertia and the pressure of vested interest that ensure continuity in existing expenditure patterns.

When the IAP was launched in 1977 there existed a very different climate for public expenditure, particularly in local government. Although coming under increasing scrutiny, there was still sufficient growth in main programme budgets to permit some experimentation and service development. When budgets were expanding, even marginally, they permitted an element of flexibility in policies which was crucial to the success of the IAP. An element of growth was vital to enable both the redirection of expenditure to areas of special need and to permit time-expired IAP projects to be taken onto main programmes at the end of their funding period.

The redirection in public expenditure after 1979 undermined the IAP in two ways. Firstly, the IAP lost much of its credibility with officers and members alike. The commitment in the White Paper to an 'explicit priority' to be given to the inner cities in the programme of central government departments never materialized and instead the massive cuts imposed on local authority expenditure outweighed the value of the IAP.

In such circumstances, it has become increasingly difficult for either the DoE or local authorities to enforce the pioneering spirit of *Policy for the Inner Cities* on harassed departments. As a result of the cuts, the experimental role of the IAP has been quietly forgotten as chief officers and members have turned to the IAP to supplement deficiencies in main programme funding. This can be seen clearly in the use made of the IAP for housing policy and expenditure in Leicester. As one senior officer acknowledged, the IAP was 'Not really a source of ideas, it merely provided us with the cash to enable us to do things.'

The principal housing activity supported through the IAP in Leicester has been the provision of hostels for groups of people defined as being in 'special need'. In the three years from 1979 to 1982, two-thirds of the projects and half of the total housing expenditure in the IAP were devoted to hostel accommodation. The Housing Department recognized that this was 'an unimaginative use' of the IAP funds but justified it in terms of the current resource position. The IAP had enabled the department to 'get things through' for which they would not otherwise have had the resources.

The second major way in which public expenditure cuts have undermined the IAP is in questioning the wisdom and purpose of experimentation itself. Could chief officers really justify cutting back main programme activities in order to find their committee's 25 per cent contribution to support an experimental or marginal IAP project? Establishing an experimental project often has long-term resource implications for a department. Is it responsible, for example, to set up an experimental project which may reveal hidden need if the resources are not there in main programme budgets to meet it?

In a climate of cuts, is experimentation either feasible or responsible? Can the increased manpower necessary to monitor schemes be justified if there is little possibility of the lessons learnt being applied in a wider context? Does the IAP merely highlight areas of need or deficiencies in services which cannot be met? Unless there is some commitment to tackling the issues raised by experimental projects, there is little point in experimentation for its own sake.

The second major constraint on innovation in the IAP has been the rules and regulations imposed by the DoE, which have exerted a massive bias to any possible learning process. For public learning to occur, there needs to be a structured format within which the experimentation process can be applied. Thought needs to be given as to what are the major areas in which action research could be useful. Thus, for one department the issue of service provision for ethnic minority groups may be a pressing problem, whilst for another the IAP could provide resources to enter a new field of activity, such as the provision of a welfare rights service. In each case the 'action' is not just an end in itself, but provides an input into the monitoring process. The problem here, as we have seen, is that the rules that the DoE have imposed upon the IAP have, in effect, reduced it to an annual allocation exercise, in which local authorities attempt to balance their programme to meet DoE guidelines, rather than determining their own priorities. So there is an enormous bias built into the IAP process which works against its use as a vehicle for experimentation.

It is difficult to conceive of a set of rules and regulations which would be less conducive to experimentation than that which governs the IAP. Whilst *Policy for the Inner Cities* saw local authorities as 'the natural agencies to tackle inner area problems' the element of local discretion in the IAP has been considerably reduced in recent years. The DoE has issued a series of guidelines to local authorities which recommend particular desired proportions in the IAP expenditure both between capital and revenue expenditure and also between the economic, environmental and social projects to be included. In essence the government now wishes to encourage capital expenditure on economic projects whilst many local authorities place priority on social projects, which often have a high revenue element. The effect of the government's policy of management by cash controls is such that, for local authorities, the policy element in the IAP has been subverted by the need to assemble a suitably balanced programme. Thus, in the selection process not all projects are treated equally. A project's classification (economic, environment or social) and the type of expenditure required (capital or revenue) is a major factor in determining how likely it is to receive funding. In such circumstances the innovatory or experimental potential of a project ranks fairly low on the assessment criteria.

The second major financial constraint on experimentation in the IAP is section 137 of the 1972 Local Government Act. This enables local authorities to levy up to a 2p rate to finance schemes which fall outside their normal statutory responsibilities, but which are deemed by the authority to be of benefit to the local community. The IAP presents a major challenge, especially to non-metropolitan district authorities, in finding their 25 per cent share of the IAP funding. Many projects, especially those which are experimental, fall outside the authorities' normal responsibilities. In such cases, section 137 is virtually the only avenue available for local authorities to raise the necessary finance. Thus, some authorities, such as Leicester City Council, have found that as they finance more and more IAP schemes they are reaching the limit of their section 137 allowance. It is ironic that local authorities have the powers to finance IAP projects which *do* fall under their main programme responsibilities but increasingly *do not* have the finance for more experimental schemes.

This provides a clear example of an inconsistency in government policy which on the one hand seeks to encourage innovation whilst on the other denies local authorities the resources to do so. Yet the responsibility for preparing an IAP rests with the programme authority. It is, therefore, up to the programme authority to set the research agenda; identifying the problems it wishes to explore, inviting and then selecting projects to tackle these problems and monitoring the results. If learning is to take place in anything more than an *ad hoc* way it is the programme authority that must be willing to take the lead.

We have suggested that if experimentation and monitoring in the IAP are taken at face value, as a genuine attempt at public learning, it would encounter serious problems. In addition to the usual technical and political difficulties surrounding evaluation exercises, we have seen that both the rules that govern the IAP and the massive cuts in public expenditure have effectively undermined the possibility of using the IAP in an experimental way.

Summary

We have seen that at every stage the planning cycle of the IAP has experienced major difficulties. These have been both conceptual (what is the IAP? what is it trying to do?) and practical (the problems of attempting to secure agreement to common objectives between different agencies). In addition the difficulties encountered in programming have been compounded for the IAP by the financial strait-jacket imposed by the government guidelines. The combined result of these factors has been to reduce the IAP to an annual resource allocation exercise concerned with a limited, but still useful, grant-aided programme. Now any pretence at involving main programme expenditure has been dropped.

As councils wrestle with the problems of severe public expenditure cuts they do not have the resources available to redirect their main programmes in favour of the inner cities, even if the IAP provided sufficient theoretical justification why they should do so (which it does not), or if there was a general political commitment in favour of such a redirection (which there is not).

5 Local economic policies: reversing the 'engines of exodus'?

Introduction

A central thread of urban policy has always addressed the problems of local economic decline. Local authorities have been involved in economic development for many years, but their role expanded and diversified in the mid-1970s. This enhanced local economic development function was legitimated by Circular 71/77 (DoE 1977a), 'Local Government and the Industrial Strategy'. In the ten years since the IAP was established, the local economic development function has ultimately become clearly articulated through inner cities policy and through the IAP in particular. To what extent can the IAP achieve the economic regeneration of the inner cities, which is at the heart of its intentions, and what are the dilemmas created in its attempts at local economic initiatives?

This chapter looks at the development of local economic and employment activity since 1976/7 and its relationship with the IAP. It examines the background to local economic policy formulation and outlines the growing criticisms of 'traditional' economic initiatives as failing to address the employment needs of local areas. It goes on to assess the set of local economic and employment initiatives which together have been developed by left-wing Labour-controlled councils as part of their package of activities to promote 'Municipal Socialism'. Recent critiques of these policies as limited in their impact largely to the political, rather than to the economic, sphere are examined, using case study material from the key Labour left councils including Leicester City Council. Finally, we examine the impact of the IAP itself on the development and implementation of local economic policy and assess the extent to which the IAP acts as a brake on more radical and experimental initiatives.

Local economic initiatives – the policy framework

With soaring unemployment levels since the 1970s, local authorities have become increasingly concerned with local economic and employment policies. The de-industrialization of manufacturing-based conurbations in the UK, together with central government industrial policy, which has been aimed increasingly at letting the market restructure industry regardless of the consequences for employment, has put local authorities under pressure to extend the scope and scale of their own policies for the local economy. This section examines the broad range of local initiatives currently being pursued in local authorities around the country, from the traditional site assembly/infrastructure provision, which is now an established feature of mainstream local government activity, to the more interventionist strategies which have been pursued in several Labour authorities, most notably Sheffield City Council, the old GLC and West Midlands County Council.

This expansion of local government activity in the economic sphere has occurred at a time when the economic and political relationship between central and local government has been in a period of rapid change. From 1980 onwards, central government has viewed the control of local government expenditure as a central element of its general policy of reducing public expenditure. Through the introduction of the block grant system, which penalized overspending councils by the withdrawal of grant aid, and more recently the rate-capping of authorities who attempted to carry on spending by making up the lost income from the rates, central government has undermined local government's ability to set its own budget. Politically, the past eight years have seen repeated attempts by central government to proscribe the activities at local government level through expenditure controls, and where this has proved to have only limited success, it has circumvented local councils altogether, for example establishing enterprise zones, urban development corporations and task forces. This chapter shows how this changing central–local relation influenced the characteristics of local economic policy as councils had to use the limited source of finance available to them and made use of funds such as the IAP.

The growing interest in recent attempts by local authorities to promote industrial growth or arrest economic decline has tended

to obscure the historic concern of both local and central governments with industrial and economic policy (Young, Mason and
Mills 1980). It is important to understand the broad policies
pursued at both local and central government level, as these form
the basic policy framework within which a single local authority
has to formulate its own particular initiatives. Until 1979, two
main types of policy were being pursued by central government.
Sectoral policy was manifest explicitly through industrial strategy
and implicitly through the control of nationalized industries.
Spatial policy was being pursued via regional policy, New Towns
policy, urban policy and locational policies for replacing obsolete
plant with new investment, promoting economies of scale, encouraging the demise of inefficient firms and the location of new
investment on 'green-field' sites, in new settlements or on the
fringes of existing settlements (Davies 1980). With the rise of
unemployment in the mid-1970s, job creation policies came to the
fore, but these were largely concerned with providing alternative
initiatives for the unemployed rather than with improving the
performance of industry. Policy was concerned more with picking
up the pieces of industrial change than with strengthening the
economic base.

There has been considerable debate about the effectiveness of
these various policies: some say that they have merely facilitated
the process of industrial decentralization, which would have
happened anyway (Massey 1978); others say that without these
policies the economy would be worse off than it is now (Moore
and Rhodes 1979). Their effect has been most severe amongst
older firms and plants in the inner city areas, given that these tend
to be the least modern, least efficient and least competitive.

In the face of this central government policy, which has tended
to reinforce rather than to counteract inner city de-industrialization, the economic activities of local authorities have become
increasingly important. Not that local authority activity in this
field is new: a good deal of nineteenth- and early twentieth-century
municipal enterprise was directed precisely at improving the economic well-being of local areas, and before the First World War
urban politics often turned on arguments about the impact of local
policies on the urban economy. Between the wars a large number
of local authorities were involved in industrial development and
their activities received a certain amount of encouragement from
central government as 'self-help' schemes (Young, Mason and

Mills 1980). Although in the immediate post-war period national government policies overshadowed the role of local authorities in the field of industrial attraction and development, by the late 1950s there was a revival of the economic role of local government. Since local government reorganization this role has been taken further. The continuing economic crisis and the consequent high levels of unemployment have encouraged more local authorities to follow the innovators, and since the late 1970s there has been a dramatic increase both in the number of authorities giving priority to industrial development and in the range of activities they are carrying out (CLES 1986; Gaunt 1982).

The encouragement given to local economic policy by Circular 71/77 (DoE 1977a) and the impact of the UP, expanded and recast as the IAP in 1977, encouraged and sustained local authority involvement in industrial development. It increased the resources available to IAP authorities, expanding the scale of activity and the range of activities involved. Drawing on evidence from the Inner Area Studies research, the White Paper *Policy for the Inner Cities* acknowledged for the first time in UK urban policy that 'the decline in the economic fortunes of the inner areas often lies at the heart of the problem of urban deprivation' (para. 7).

Of the four underlying aims set out in the White Paper, two concerned employment and the economy:

a strengthening the economies of the inner areas and the prospects of their residents, and
b securing a new balance between the inner areas and the rest of the city region in terms of population and jobs. (para. 26)

Under the heading of 'Improving Social Conditions', the White Paper stated that 'The relief of unemployment and the provision of decent jobs with good wages would go a long way towards dealing with poverty and raising morale' (para. 29).

The government's proposals, which included the concept of 'bending' main programmes, gave immediate priority to the strengthening of the inner cities' economies. Thus the government perceived the employment and economic aspects of the new policy to be central to the success of the programme. Over time, as the IAP has given much greater priority to economic measures and more authorities have received assistance as partnership and programme authorities, so the IAP has acted as a very important stimulant to the development of economic initiatives in urban areas.

Nevertheless, whilst fostering local economic initiatives in this way, central government has sought to increase its control over partnership and programme authorities by means of guidelines that regulate the type of economic projects appropriate for urban programme funding (DoE 1981). Most recently, the Urban Programme Management Initiative (UPMI) has required authorities to set targets and output measures relating to their programme for the approval of the DoE. With the enhanced emphasis on the private sector in urban policy, it is clear that central government has sought both to encourage and manage the relationship between local authorities and the private sector.

Despite these centralizing tendencies, Labour-controlled authorities have been particularly keen to develop strong local employment and economic policies, using whatever funds available, in response to rising unemployment which Conservative administrations have viewed as an essential, though temporary, part of the restructuring of capital in the UK. The years since the general election of 1979 have brought to power Labour Party branches committed to an explicit form of local socialism. The development of radical employment policies by these Labour councils is a central plank in their overall socialist strategy, and the policies have been as much about 'propaganda by example' as about purely economic considerations, as this chapter goes on to discuss.

Thus a number of distinct strands came together in the early 1980s to produce the range of local authority economic and employment policies which are now an important feature of local government activity. Rising unemployment nationally was prompting local demands for positive action in areas most affected by industrial decline. At the same time the powers and resources available to local authorities to intervene in the economy had been extended by central government policy in the late 1970s. In particular the UP had been recast from a social to an essentially economic policy framework and the new corporate structures set up after local government reorganization in 1974. Although the new Thatcher administration at first attempted to reduce expenditure on urban policy and curtail the use of section 137 money by local authorities, the riots of 1981 and the effects of Michael Heseltine's initiatives in Liverpool renewed the government's commitment to inner city policy. However, the policy was refocused on the economic aspects, with an increased emphasis on capital rather than revenue-oriented schemes.

At the same time, regional and industrial aid was being severely cut in real terms. In addition, a new breed of left-wing Labour councils were formed which wanted to challenge the economic policies of a Conservative government with alternative local economic strategies based on socialist principles. Not that left-wing councils had the monopoly on local economic initiatives of course, for a striking feature of local government activity over the last ten to fifteen years has been the increase in economic and employment activity in local councils of all political persuasions. Nevertheless, the left-wing authorities have been particularly interventionist in this field of activity and have developed strategies and initiatives which are qualitatively new and different from the more traditional economic development activities now pursued in the majority of British authorities. We will now turn to the range of 'mainstream' local economic policies before looking in more detail at the radical employment plans of the left-wing councils.

Shifting deckchairs on the *Titanic*: traditional local economic policies

The range and scale of local authority economic policies are extensive, with some authorities keeping a low profile whilst others pursue ambitious interventionist strategies. Nevertheless, even passive local authorities have an impact on the local economy in a variety of ways, including direct employment, purchasing goods and services, providing land, premises and infrastructure to businesses, education and training, planning policies, providing financial assistance to small firms, giving business advice and information, industrial promotion campaigns, and working with the unemployed, community groups, trade unions, etc.

By its existence, the local authority has a major influence upon the economy of the local area, even if this is not explicitly recognized by the authority itself. Marshall and Mawson (1984) have outlined four major factors which help explain the particular direction a local authority may take with regard to economic and employment policies. These factors are: the nature of the local economic problems; the resources available; the organizational structure of the authority; and finally, its politcal direction.

1. *The nature of the local economic problem.* Each area of the country has different local economic and employment problems. The corporate structure of the local economy is also a major influence on the types of policies the local authority will need to adopt, for example, support for many small firms or intervention in one major sector or firm; training for local skill shortages or helping to develop cooperative and other forms of local enterprise. The different sorts of economic problems being faced in different areas impose varying constraints upon, and present different opportunities for, the emegence of local economic initiatives.

2. *The resources available to a local authority.* The availability of resources poses a major constraint on local authorities' ability to pursue their economic and employment objectives. The smaller authorities face the greatest constraints in this respect because their rate base is smaller. Economic and employment activity is not part of a local authority's statutory responsibilities, but by using resources raised under section 137 of the 1972 Local Government Act, a local authority can spend up to 2p in the pound of its rateable income on such non-statutory activities. For district authorities the product of section 137 may be relatively small, and where it is also used to fund other activities (e.g. supporting voluntary sector projects) this can act as a major constraint on ambitious economic plans. There are other funds which can be used, including: urban programme funding, which has increasingly become an economic programme; regional policy funding in designated areas; EEC funds in certain areas; Manpower Services Commission (MSC) resources for training places, where the local authority can provide the initial start-up capital and equipment costs of a project whilst the MSC pays for the staff; and finally, several authorities are investigating the use of their pension funds.

3. *The organizational structure of the local authority.* Economic and employment activities in local authorities typically straddle the traditional responsibilities of several departments (e.g. estates, planning, employment, etc.). The extent to which local authorities have evolved an organizational structure which can accommodate and encourage the corporate development of this new policy area is a significant factor in explaining the type of economic activity undertaken. Despite reorganization in 1974, the majority of local authorities still have a departmenta-

lized rather than a corporate structure. This has frequently meant that the different departments have taken on responsibility for implementing different aspects of economic and employment development activity, leading in many cases to inconsistencies in policy and to a fragmented and uncoordinated approach. Indeed, recent studies have shown that it is a mistake to assume that all the principal decision-makers in local authorities share a common view of the desirability of the local authority economic role, not least because of the different perspectives generated by professional training. Within authorities, it is frequently the case that estates and industrial development officers feel that their own work is legitimate, but that the 'soft' end of policy, such as schemes to help particular disadvantaged groups in the labour market, is quite outside the proper scope of local authority work. The problem is often reinforced by the organizational separation which exists in most authorities between those concerned with the regeneration aspects of economic and employment policy (estates officers, physical planners, industrial development and promotion officers) and those concerned with the disadvantaged in the labour market (employment policy units, careers advisers, voluntary sector coordinators, etc.) (Davies 1980; Marshall and Mawson 1984; Young and Mason 1983). Of course, alongside this, there are authorities which have developed a strong, corporate direction to policy, using economic and employment units based in Chief Executive's Departments. However, even where policy *formulation* is coordinated and developed centrally, policy *implementation* may still be fragmented.

4. *Political direction*. In many authorities the commitment to economic and, particularly, unemployment initiatives, has come principally from members. If there is a clear political vision of what type of strategy is to be pursued by an authority, this will have a major impact on the actual policies implemented. However, there is often a strategic vacuum within which policies arise on an *ad hoc* basis, either following initiatives taken by individual officers or departments, or under the influence of external programmes such as the IAP or the MSC's special measures.

Thus there are a number of key factors which influence the types of economic and employment policy pursued by different local authorities. Most councils' policies, however, are restricted to activity in land and premises, to advertising and promotional work aimed at new and expanding firms, to providing loans and/ or grants and advice to businesses. As Goodwin and Duncan (1985) have said, this form of local economic activity is 'little more than hopeful persuasion and petty bribery' (p. 246).

These traditional forms of local economic development activity have been roundly criticized by many commentators, politicians and local authority officers concerned with local economic regeneration. Despite these criticisms, these policies continue to proliferate. Policy inertia explains much of the current activity in the more traditional forms of local economic development as these are well established activities which departments are able to undertake quite routinely. These policies also have the advantage of being publicly visible with something being 'seen to be done'. The 'symbolic reassurance' we have seen earlier as a crucial factor underlying specifically the IAP is no less important in the context of local economic and employment initiatives.

Most commentators now agree that these interventions can only have, at best, a minor effect and they can even make things worse. The limitations of these types of activity have been extensively reviewed by Cochrane (1985). They point to the futility of local authorities spending a great deal of time and money competing with each other to attract small or 'footloose' firms to relocate to their area – job redistribution rather than job creation. Many apparent success stories will actually describe firms that would have moved anyway, as part of their own restructuring strategy, rather than because of local economic policy. As Martin Boddy (1984) has argued 'Competing in a limited market and duplicating expenditure on promotion, provision of sites and premises has undoubtedly been wasteful and inefficient, at best shifting jobs around like deckchairs on the *Titanic* rather than sustaining real economic growth' (p. 16).

The West Midlands County Council, for example, estimated that it would take mobile plants on the scale of 260 Nissans, 500 Commodores or 26 000 new small firms to replace the jobs lost in the traditional metal manufacturing sector in the region; it was for that reason that its own emphasis was on the promotion of indigenous industry and on assisting *existing* firms (usually medium and large sized) rather than trying to attract new ones through large advertising campaigns.

In part this move to assist medium and large firms has been based on a growing critique of those mainstream policies which give advice, encouragement and support to small firms. The latter half of the 1980s has seen the gradual erosion of the 'small firm myth', the belief that if 'enterprise' in the community was released and enough new small firms were set up, then this would significantly lower unemployment levels, particularly in the cities. In fact, there is now a wealth of empirical evidence showing that small firms are ineffectual in providing alternative employment on the scale necessary to replace those lost from the closure of larger firms in an area (see Storey 1985). Jobs created in small firms tend to be marginal, short-lived, low paid, tied to the subcontract of a large firm, in contrast to the populist 'silicon valley', 'high-tech' view of the small entrepreneur.

Thus mainstream local economic policies have been 'property-led business and market-oriented, and competitive with economic development rather than employment as the primary focus' (Boddy, 1984, pp. 163–4). It is for these reasons primarily that a growing number of Labour-controlled local authorities have developed their own, more radical policies. It is, however, understandable that many local authorities have been reluctant to embark wholesale on new and untried employment projects when whole departments exist with a history of expertise in traditional schemes. As Stewart and Underwood (1983) have argued in the specific context of economic policies in programme authorities: 'the inner cities programme and the aspirations towards innovation, experimentation and support for non-traditional activity has tended to legitimate and sanction many of the existing economic development activities already being planned or carried out (p. 149).

Employment-related policies may also appear as 'soft' options to those concerned with the private market and property within the authority, and outside it such policies may be questioned as a legitimate use of public money: 'pump-priming' may be seen as legitimate but 'handouts' are not. Overall, there is typically an underlying assumption that the employment benefits of site assembly and factory unit provision, infrastructure projects and industrial promotion will simply follow on automatically from these activities. The link between economic policy and the labour market is taken for granted, based on the assumption that the benefits of economic development will simply trickle down into the labour market. As Davies (1980) points out, however, research evidence shows that such a link, if it is there at all, is not automatic, and indeed that there are some disadvantaged groups in the labour market (ethnic minorities, women, the disabled, the low-skilled) who are likely to remain bypassed by general economic development unless policies are directed specifically at them.

This problem has been typified as the market versus welfare dichotomy: should local authorities be concerned with the issue of market facilitation and underwriting the costs of private investment (through site assembly and infrastructure projects, finance, etc.) or should they be concerned with the employment and welfare needs of its residents (Young and Mason 1983)? The radical economic and employment strategies now being pursued in several Labour-controlled local authorities are, in part, an attempt to integrate the more traditional market concerns of local economic activity with welfare concerns, by challenging the existing relations between capital and labour and by integrating specific employment issues (including conditions and wages) with wider economic development activities. A phrase widely used to sum up these radical initiatives is 'restructuring for labour, not capital'.

How different then are these new radical economic policies from the traditional ones outlined in this section, and how successful have they been in challenging capital–labour relations and restructuring 'for labour'?

Radical economic and employment policies: restructuring for Labour?

In the early 1980s, a number of Labour-controlled local councils began to develop alternative economic strategies which went beyond traditional mainstream policy concerns. As unemployment levels rose dramatically, the limitations of mainstream policies became increasingly obvious and demands for a more directed set of economic policies, based on maintaining and increasing employment opportunities and on economic regeneration in local economies grew. The 'broad-brush' policies involving councils giving conventional aid to firms in their eagerness to attract any jobs to their area were critically examined and more authorities became willing not only to insist that conditions were attached to aid but also to make decisions as to which sort of firms should be encouraged in this way. More attention was paid to ways in which existing, indigenous industry could be retained and supported in contrast to approaches which emphasized promotion and attracting new firms. In addition, the quality and type of employment thus retained or created became for the first time a central consideration in the policy planning process.

A hallmark of local economic policy in these authorities has been the recognition of the need to receive an input from a broad range of groups including trade unions, the voluntary sector, the cooperative movement etc. Those involved in the grass roots of the Labour movement produced a critical review of Labour's industrial policies which argued for increased democracy and increased worker participation in the decisions of the public and private sectors of both industry and government. This push for democracy in local economic planning led to the emergence of 'popular planning' units, typified in approach by that in Ken Livingstone's GLC (Mackintosh and Wainright 1987).

The left Labour employment policies were also expected to provide concrete examples of the type of activity that a future Labour government should be trying to foster. Local initiatives were seen as prefiguring future national policies and enabling the benefits of radical Labour policies to be seen and enjoyed in the present, even if a Labour government was unlikely to be elected for several years. The notion of 'propaganda by example' was then at the forefront of these new initiatives. The left-wing Labour councils pursuing such strategies clearly have given themselves a lot to live up to. So what sort of radical new initiatives have they actually implemented? We can pick out four key areas of activity which typify the general approach taken by the left councils although, it must be noted, each authority does pursue different strategies according to the needs of the local economy. These four areas are: selective financial assistance to firms, based on strategic research and monitoring of the local economy; integrating welfare considerations, such as low pay, with the wider economic strategy; using the authority's leverage as a major purchaser in the local economy; and establishing enterprise boards. These can now be considered in turn.

Selective financial assistance to key sectors

A key feature of the radical authorities' economic strategies is that they are typically informed by active research and intelligence activity which provides the necessary information about the local economy and labour market and which also places their economic policies within the wider national and international economic context. It is not the case that any job is better than no job: their aim is that research should identify strategic sectors where investment will maximize the future economic development potential of local industry. Action research is often an associated feature of this activity, working with unions in campaigns and preparing proposals, and providing political and financial support for groups of workers trying to defend their jobs.

Assistance which is provided to the private sector usually takes the form of direct intervention using the leverage of finance and other forms of assistance to achieve the precise economic and social objectives, rather than providing general non-selective assistance. Assistance in the form of grants and loans is targeted at particular types or sizes of firms according to defined criteria, together with certain conditions of assistance which are typically attached. Thus, for example, at the Greater London Council assistance was targeted at particular industrial sectors, such as clothing and furniture, which were seen as meeting the basic needs of Londoners; at particular types of firm, such as cooperatives and community businesses which related to the GLC's wider political objectives of influencing the process of economic change in London; at particular parts of London, such as those experiencing severe social deprivation; and at particular groups in the community, such as young people, ethnic minorities and the unskilled who were identified as experiencing particular disadvantages in the labour market.

In the West Midlands, the county council's private sector initiatives were geared to investing funds in medium-sized enterprises where the prospects for using public money as a lever to secure additional funds, as well as making a long-term contribution to employment in the area, was greatest. In addition, the council concentrated its investments on equity holdings which effectively reduced the assisted companies gearing ratios of share loans and capital, facilitating further access to sources of loan finance while providing the council with a degree of influence over the firms' activities. Similarly, Sheffield City Council shifted its emphasis away from an 'open-door' approach to financial assistance to one where support is given to key industries and certain categories of enterprise, in return for them signing a planning agreement.

Integrating welfare and market concerns

Radical economic strategies have been used to link social objectives to wider economic goals. Policies have been targeted at certain disadvantaged groups, such as ethnic minorities, women and the disabled. There has been concern over the conditions and pay associated with the jobs retained or created through the economic policies, and attempts have been made to promote forms of work which fulfil certain social objectives and which increase workers' control over their jobs, e.g. cooperatives and community businesses. In addition, the notion of 'socially useful production' has become important, involving the production of goods which people in the community want, as exemplified by the Lucas Aerospace alternative production plan. In this context, work with trade unions has been of particular importance.

A particular concern in this field is that of low pay and welfare rights. It is increasingly argued that low pay and conditions at work are an entirely legitimate and important concern of authorities' wider employment policies, and that for the unemployed and the low paid, welfare benefits advice is a vital resource. Thus in the West Midlands the county council has developed a community strategy aimed at alleviating the effects of recession and restructuring on working people. This strategy has involved training measures, welfare benefit take-up initiatives, attacking illegal low pay, providing counselling and work opportunities for the unemployed and assisting voluntary groups. The more radical councils have also funded unemployed workers' centres in conjunction with local trades councils and several Trade Union Resource Centres have also been set up with local authority financial support.

However, there are two main difficulties for local authorities attempting to integrate welfare and market objectives. The first is the increasing realization that supporting enterprises which have 'social objectives' on a commercial basis frequently proves to be a very expensive option, as the next section goes on to discuss in some detail. Secondly, however, conflicts within central government have caused problems for local councils attempting to target employment initiatives at particular local groups. Of particular importance here was the conflict between Kenneth Clarke, MP, and Nicholas Ridley, MP, which emerged in 1987 over contract compliance: At the Department of the Environment Ridley wanted to outlaw all forms of contract compliance in his new Local Government Bill, while at the Department of Employment Clarke argued the case for local councils having the right to insist that *local* people were employed on certain community building and renovation projects.

The local authority's leverage within the local economy

Radical councils have recognized that the authority's role as a major employer and purchaser gives it important leverage in the local economy. Marginal changes to the pattern and level of local authorities' main programme spending may actually have a much greater impact upon employment in the locality than the specific economic initiatives they pursue, in the short term at least. The important role an authority plays within the local labour market is thus a central concern of wider economic and employment strategy. Several authorities have developed policies, for example, to increase the number of women and ethnic minority craft apprentices in their direct labour organizations in addition to the general equal opportunities policies to make council jobs at all levels more accessible for women, the disabled and ethnic minority applicants. The establishment of contracts compliance policies and units to administer and monitor these has been another feature in several Labour-controlled authorities.

Enterprise boards

Local authority development companies, of which enterprise boards are one variation, are not new; originally they were set up primarily for land development purposes but were given new impetus with the imposition of central government capital controls in 1981, when some local authorities realized that they could set up separate independent companies where funds could be redirected and thus bypass central government controls. Not all the Labour-controlled interventionist authorities have chosen to set up enterprise boards, however; Sheffield City Council took the decision *not* to set one up, maintaining that it can undertake virtually all the activities of an enterprise board without the need to set up a separate company, and in so doing can retain full and direct control over economic development.

The enterprise boards all had initial funding from their 'parent' authorities. In the case of the West Midlands Enterprise Board (WMEB) this amounted to £4 million and the Greater London Enterprise Board (GLEB) had an initial budget of £35 million for 1982–3 and a further £32 million for 1983–4 from the GLC's section 137 funds. Efforts are also made to 'lever' finance from other public and private sector organizations, including pension funds, banks and insurance companies and the Industrial Commercial Finance Corporation (ICFC).

It would be wrong to suggest, however, that all the enterprise boards followed the same principles. In particular, there is the question of whether the enterprise boards are simply 'lubricating the capitalist system' and contributing to the better management of capitalist enterprises: municipal capitalism or municipal socialism?

The arguments are highlighted by the operations of the two largest boards, WMEB and GLEB. The WMEB's role is defined as a public sector development capital company. It aims to step in and provide financial assistance of the right type to companies going into receivership because of shortage of capital, or being closed down through company reorganization. Some of these may remain viable as individual units, but not as profitable as other units in the company or may not fit into wider corporate plans. Development capital is defined in this respect as finance used by established firms to restructure themselves or promote expansion. The GLEB, however, has rejected the conventional interpretation of an equity gap in the capital market. It sees the problem of underinvestment as arising not from shortage of capital but from an absence of acceptable outlets for private investors who are drawn into short-term lending, often overseas, in preference to longer term investments in domestic industry. The GLEB argues that attempts by the local authority to fulfil any deficiency in the capital markets will not necessarily fulfil the council's economic and employment objectives. The GLEB views its financing role simply as an opportunity to intervene directly in the process of capital restructuring in the interests of labour, rather than as a source of development capital for local businesses.

Radical economic policies: propaganda by example or an example of propaganda?

What, then, has been the effect of these new radical policies? Their proponents have certainly claimed a great deal for them. Michael Ward, former Chair of the GLC's Economic Development Committee and now Director of the Centre for Local Economic Studies has, for example, claimed that: 'Local initiatives can demonstrate that the alternative works; that greater democratic control and the planned use of resources can be used to create jobs. Local initiatives can lay out the line of policy that a future Labour government can follow' (Ward 1981).

Clearly, success *in practice* would be a stronger justification of local economic policy than the propaganda of words. However, precisely what this 'alternative' means *in practice* remains unclear. Have the radical economic policies pursued in the past seven or eight years by left local authorities really succeeded not only within their political terms of reference but also their economic terms? Has the democratization of local economic development plans and the new emphasis on the *quality* of employment been matched by the creation and preservation of jobs?

Evaluating public policies, and particularly local economic and employment policies, is notoriously difficult. It is often impossible to tell what would have happened in the absence of the policy. Nevertheless, there is a growing body of criticism over the policies to 'restructure for labour'. Has local economic activity merely become the playground of the new left?

If radical strategies are to command and build credibility, resources and political backing, it is important that they are seen to be at least as effective on the same terms as mainstream approaches (Boddy 1984). More explicitly, Duncan and Goodwin (1985) have argued that

In the end these Councils' actions may only differ from traditional economic policies to the extent that they avoid the worst cases of worker and area exploitation, refrain from direct poaching, and strengthen both worker organizations and public accountability at the margins. The overall economic effect will still be small. An improvement, certainly, but not socially-based economic regeneration. (p. 20)

What then, is the evidence of the economic success of the radical policies and what are the major problems they have faced in attempting to challenge capital and restructure for labour?

Job losses at the local level are part of a wider, international process of industrial restructuring which has been exacerbated by central government monetarist policies. Against this background, there are obviously major limitations on what a single local authority can achieve within the local economy, particularly in the short term; resources are severely constrained, local authorities do not have the same powers to undertake economic planning as central government and they have even less power to influence the investment decisions of multinational firms whose branch plants are located in the local economy than central government.

The number of jobs created or retained as a result of local authority economic policies inevitably appears insignificant against the rising tide of unemployment. In its first two years, for example, the GLEB claimed to have saved or created 2000 jobs at an average direct investment cost per job of £11 000. This is in comparison to the estimated £35 000 cost per job of national regional policy and £68 000 per job for the government's enterprise zone scheme. GLEB's interventions would at first glance appear to be clearly cost-effective. But the jobs created or retained by them need to be seen in the context of the 400 000 unemployed in London in 1985 (GLC 1985).

The GLEB is the only enterprise board with really large financial resources to spend (£40 million from section 137). However, more recent evidence suggests that the GLEB's interventions in the London economy were nowhere near as successful as first claimed. Of the 279 investments made by the GLEB in 1983/4 and 1984/5, only forty-one firms remained in operation at the demise of the GLC in 1986. These forty-one had an estimated asset value of only £1.5 million, despite an injection of £14.8 million from the GLEB. In total 465 associated jobs were still in existence in 1986. Furthermore, these jobs tended to be low paid, low skilled jobs; employment conditions were poor and the traditional division of labour (i.e. women occupying the most menial and poorest paid jobs) had rarely been altered (Welbur 1987).

In the West Midlands, by comparison, section 137 funds only raise some £8 million. Attempts to increase financial resources by using pension funds have been thwarted by legislative and political obstacles, so that West Midlands County Council has not been able to use even its own pension fund for local investment with over £500 million in 1982). In 1983–4 the WMEB had an investment portfolio of £5.2 million, supporting 1700 jobs: this obviously represents a beginning, but these jobs nevertheless are only a drop in the ocean compared to the overall economic changes and job loss in the West Midlands since 1981.

Similarly, the number of jobs created by Sheffield City Council between 1981 and 1984 was estimated at 1000, which only matched the number of jobs lost *each month* of that three-year period (Child and Paddon 1984). With limited resources (in Sheffield the product of the 2p rate under section 137 produces only £1.8 million) the council found that its activities were peripheral to Sheffield's unemployment problem and declining industrial structure.

The jobs which have been saved or created as a direct result of the activities of the Labour left councils' economic strategies are obviously the main 'success' by which these policies can be judged. Nevertheless, welcome as these jobs are, they are still dwarfed by the scale of urban deincustrialization and inner city unemployment. A key problem is the conflict between the aims of ensuring that the jobs created or retained are 'good' jobs, with proper rates of pay and good conditions, and the exigencies of the capitalist market-place. For example, Sheffield City Council intervened in a firm in the cutlery sector which was economically backward and which was surviving by virtue of its low pay rates. Enforcing higher rates without economic and technical restructuring would threaten jobs, but restructuring would improve competitiveness and so threaten other firms in Sheffield. The other interventionist councils have faced similar dilemmas.

A related problem which has been raised is the possibility of building an alternative economic strategy on the basis of rescue attempts on failing capitalist firms. The firms which approach left-wing councils for financial assistance are unlikely to be highly successful or in a leading position within their sectors; yet it would clearly be much easier to build a socialist economic strategy using successful enterprises. Failing firms which need assistance from local authorities may never succeed, despite all the financial and management help they can be offered. If they have had bad management, failed to adapt to the market, failed to innovate or to invest sufficiently, these firms may simply not have the potential to develop into sound economic enterprises. An example here would be the West Midlands County Council's support for

Meriden motorcycles, which eventually went into receivership. In this case, the district auditor's investigations led to the threat of court action against the chief economist of the economic development unit for misusing ratepayers' money. The threatened court action never took place. For local authorities with very limited financial resources, investing in failing companies may be risky and lead to expensive mistakes. This problem has been recognized by authorities such as Sheffield City Council, which is now shifting its investment priorities much more into areas over which it has greatest control, for example its own direct labour organization, and to firms and cooperatives under direct public domination. This policy is more achievable but is also an admission of the huge limitations on local economic policies both economically and politically.

Even in the area where it is accepted that the policies of the left authorities have had an impact, that is, over the conditions of employment of workers, there are problems. Much has been made in the popular press of funding for cooperatives and community businesses. Patrick Jenkin (then Industry Minister) gave a speech to the Conservative Local Government Conference in 1982 where he spoke of putting a stop to 'authorities like the GLC pouring out thousands of pounds to their friends in Marxist co-operatives' (*New Statesman*, 14 May 1982). In practice, however, the record of cooperatives and community businesses has not been too promising, with the classic problems affecting the small firm sector in general being rife; low pay, insecurity of work, long hours and a very high failure rate in the first two years after setting up (Storey 1985). Thus despite policies for improving working practices and promoting alternative forms of ownership and control of businesses, there may be nothing intrinsically *socialist* about their outcome. So, local authority funds may end up meeting a gap in the capital market and contributing to the better management of capitalist enterprise, but this may be simply 'municipal capitalism rather than municipal socialism' (Boddy 1984, p. 181).

Finally, even the success of popular planning itself has been questioned by Mackintosh and Wainwright (1987), both of whom have an intimate knowledge of the GLC's popular planning unit. It was always the contention of the Labour left authorities, particularly in London, that even though the *outcomes* of their local economic policies would inevitably be circumscribed by the capital market they had to operate within, the *means* of formulating these policies could be harnessed in favour of working people, trade unions and local community groups, etc. Mackintosh and Wainwright, however, highlight the conflicts between different interest groups involved in the local economy, particularly with regard to issues of racism and women's rights in employment planning. The *idea* of popular planning retains its credibility, but its *practice* has been problematic.

So, to use Duncan and Goodwin's (1985) comment on radical local economic policies, 'why all the fuss?' Radical economic initiatives are most challenging at the ideological and political level, showing that there is a potential alternative to the government's policy of allowing market forces to determine the economic and employment configuration of inner cities and that local government can command the political support necessary to implement its interventionist schemes. In purely economic terms, however, we have shown that there are many factors which tend to pull back radical policies again and again to more traditional forms of activity. Behind the rhetoric, there are perhaps many more similarities between the policies implemented by the radical local authorities and the more traditional ones than there are differences.

Dave Sullivan, the Leader of the London Borough of Lewisham, recently argued that the Labour left authorities are good at devising radical policies, but not so good at implementing them. He described council activity as being like a radish, red on the outside and white and indigestible in the middle (Sullivan 1987).

Hogget (1987) has made a similar point, that radical councils have not paid enough attention to 'means' compared with the 'ends' of their radical proposals. In particular, he identifies departmentalism as a deep-seated structural obstacle to the implementation of radical policies, including economic, equal opportunity and decentralization policy. Both of these commentators, however, reinforce the argument being put here that although radical local economic policies certainly work at the symbolic level, their real impact in economic terms has yet to be proven.

But one way in which local authorities attempting to pursue more radical initiatives are forced into implementing quite traditional and mainstream activities has been virtually ignored in the now extensive literature on local economic policies. This is the impact of urban programme funding for economic initiatives. Most attention in the literature has been given, for obvious reasons to the 'market leaders' in the field of radical local economic development – the GLC, the West Midlands County Council and Sheffield City Council. Whilst the insights from these have been invaluable to other local authorities attempting to follow their lead, the emphasis on these large authorities has tended to obscure the real lack of resources faced by smaller, district authorities with a small rate base and limited functions. In these district authorities which have received UP, and particularly IAP, funding, these funds are often the major source of funding available to spend on local economic development. Table 7 charts the growth in expenditure on the economic category of the IAP in Leicester in its first five years, showing the increasing importance of this IAP funding to local economic activity.

Table 7 *Expenditure on the economic category of the IAP 1979/80 to 1983/4 in Leicester*

Year	£000s
1979/80	695.8
1980/81	1125.8
1981/82	922.3
1982/83	1127.3
1983/84	2449.0

Source: Sills, Taylor and Golding (1986)

From looking at the way in which IAP funding for economic development operates, we can see that the reliance on the IAP for such funding is a major factor leading to continued traditionalism in local economic development, whatever the rhetoric may suggest and whatever local politicians may strive for. What we can see, as the guidelines on the IAP are tightened further and further, is the emergence of a centrally controlled local economic development sector, where the policies implemented owe much more to the DoE's guidelines than to the wishes of elected councillors or, for that matter, the actual needs of the local economies in question.

We shall now look at the impact of the IAP on local economic and employment policies in more detail, drawing on our detailed research of five years of local economic policy in Leicester City Council (Sills, Taylor and Golding 1986).

Creeping traditionalism: local economic development and the IAP

This section illustrates the way in which, principally because of its internal constraints, the IAP is biased towards capital spending, physical and environmental rehabilitation schemes and projects with good spending performances. This not only flies in the face of the IAP's original conception as a source of innovative and experimental projects, but also has important consequences for local authorities who want to pursue radical economic initiatives but who are forced to rely heavily on the IAP as a major source of funding for such activity. The impact of the IAP on local economic development occurs at several levels, from the policy-making process itself through to the actual implementation of particular economic or employment schemes. Overall, though, reliance on IAP funding can act as a strong brake on local authorities wishing to pursue a radical and interventionalist local economic strategy. We can see these points clearly by looking at the relationship of the IAP to local economic development activity in Leicester.

Moves towards developing a local economic strategy in Leicester have been closely associated with the IAP in resource, organizational and political terms. The IAP for the first time offered the city council the possibility of relatively large resources to fund economic and employment-related projects. The product of section 137 funds in a small district authority such as Leicester is limited (in 1987/8, for example, Leicester City Council could spend £830 000 under section 137) and local economic development competes for what section 137 money there is with all other non-statutory activities, such as law centres, welfare rights, community groups, etc. Given this competition, IAP resources are the major source of funding by the city council for local economic development activities in Leicester. By 1984, the IAP was supporting some £2.5 million worth of economic projects, with 75 per cent of this being met by the DoE and 25 per cent by the council. This funding is not without strings, of course, and it is this which poses the problems for local economic policy development.

The second way in which the IAP has been intrinsically tied to local economic policy in Leicester has been in organizational terms. With the designation of Leicester as a programme authority in 1976 came the impetus for a number of organizational changes within the authority (Sills, Taylor and Golding 1983) which provided a useful set of corporate channels through which the economic strategy could be discussed and developed. Nationally, the IAP initiative had placed economic and employment policies at the centre of inner city regeneration. The 'economy' in its widest sense thus became one of the six key issues to be addressed by the city council through its new IAP. It was the interdepartmental working group set up to discuss this Key Issue 1 in 1979 that became the overall forum for debate on the local economy within the authority. From the outset, then, economic and employment strategy discussions within the city council centred upon the new IAP framework. It is interesting to note how the groups involved in discussing local economic policy and the IAP have changed over the years in respose to the changing perception of the local employment and economic decline. In the first year of the IAP, the Key Issue 1 Working Group was chaired by the Deputy Director of the Estates Department, the department traditionally involved in industrial development activities in the local authority. In 1980, however, the Key Issue 1 Working Group's role as the central forum for interdepartmental discussion on the local authority was taken over by the newly created Employment Liaison Group. Like the working group before it, this was also an officer group whose role was to develop policy, initiate new activities, monitor the effectiveness of projects and comment upon specific IAP bids. The Employment Liaison Group was, however, set up with a much more employment oriented brief. It was chaired not by an estates officer but by an Assistant Chief Executive, and its origins coincided with the establishment of a new Employment and Economic Development Unit (EEDU) within the Chief Executive's Department of the authority. This group used its wide brief to the full, discussing not only detailed policy recommendations for local authority activity in the economic and employment field, but also wider issues including the need to maintain the morale of the long-term unemployed, the need to promote additional further and higher educational and training opportunities and the need to recognize the long-term nature of unemployment. The group had thus progressed a long way from assessing 'traditional' economic and industrial projects. Employment issues now occupied a key place on the agenda, in contrast to the earliest years of the IAP. The 'street disturbances' of 1980 and 1981 had also made sure that the needs of the young urban unemployed were now a central area of concern. The organizational structure changed once again in 1983 when, for the first time, the political importance of local economic issues was confirmed by the setting up of three topic-based groups to replace the former issue-based groups. The topic groups (economic, environment and social) were chaired by members rather than officers and the Economic Topic Group became the focus for policy discussions on the council's economic and employment activities as well as for more detailed IAP bid evaluation.

So, in organizational terms the development of local economic and employment policy within Leicester City Council has been very closely linked to IAP mechanisms. This link has been increasingly reflected in political terms too. By 1985, the Economic and Employment Sub-Committee of the Policy and Resources Committee had actually been amalgamated with the Urban Policies Sub-Committee, reflecting the increasing formulation of the IAP as an essentially economic programme and the increasing reliance on IAP resources to fund local economic development activity. The two committees were reluctantly and temporarily separated by the ruling Labour Group after pressure from the District Labour Party in 1985, by the argument that policy development for local economic activity was being swamped by the procedures and practicalities of the IAP system. Nevertheless, tight political control and coordination of the two sub-committees was retained by means of the chair of each acting also as the vice-chair of the other committee. The decision was reversed after the local elections in 1987, reaffirming once more the strength of the links between the IAP and local economic activity in Leicester.

We can now examine further the methods by which this reliance on the IAP was translated into the 'creeping traditionalism' characteristic of local economic activity in the city. The principal factors involved are the effect of DoE guidelines on the IAP and their impact on the selection of economic projects for funding; the 'open-bidding' system of selecting individual IAP projects for funding and its deterrent to strategic decision-making; the vacuum within which decisions about local economic policy have been made; and the problems of implementation – putting the ideas into practice. The selection of IAP economic projects, and indeed, the whole development of the city council's economic and employment policy in the period 1979/80 to 1983/4 was heavily influenced by central government guidelines. As the IAP progressed, the DoE placed much more emphasis on the economic side of the programme and this had a major impact on the IAP projects selected. In 1981, DoE guidelines were issued which gave 'firm advice' on the selection of suitable projects for the IAP: programme authorities should increase their spending on economic projects in relation to social and environmental projects. The DoE had quite distinct views on what constituted an 'economic' project. The influence of this advice can be seen in the changing pattern of resources in the 1982/3 IAP, with the amount allocated to economic projects being more than double that in the 1981/2 programme (Table 8). In 1983/4 this 'guidance' had become much more a central directive which required the city council to spend 40 per cent of its total IAP on economic projects. Finally, by 1987/8, the DoE was instructing the city council to spend no more than 35 per cent of the total on social projects, and no less than 40 per cent on the economic category. The changing priorities accorded to economic projects as compared to social and environmental ones is illustrated by the figures shown in Table 8. This shows the resources Leicester City Council bid for in its annual IAP Submission Documents, and illustrates the huge increase in importance of the economic category, in line with these DoE directives.

Thus in the latter years of the IAP there was increased pressure on members and officers to select additional economic projects at the expense of more popular social projects. Not only did this mean that bids which could be put in the 'economic' category had more chance of being selected for funding than ones in the 'social' or 'environment' category, but also that economic projects were sometimes selected as *much* to 'keep up the economic side' as to meet the city council's own policy criteria developed for selecting economic bids.

The DoE guidelines influenced project selection in other ways too. Firstly, the ministerial guidelines of 1981 allowed local authorities to define the economic bids of their programmes more

Table 8 *IAP: percentage allocated to social, economic and environmental projects**

| Year | IAP category | | |
	Social %	Economic %	Environment %
1981/2	78.3	11.5	10.2
1982/3	41.0	33.0	26.0
1983/4	41.0	38.0	21.0
1984/5	36.0	40.0	24.0
1985/6	44.0	35.0	21.0
1986/7	37.0	43.0	16.0
1987/8	43.0	47.0	10.0

Source: Annual submission documents

* As given in the annual submission documents. These are the figures submitted by Leicester City Council to the DoE, not those finally approved.

widely, to include training projects and socially oriented policies to help the unemployed, such as drop-in centres. Thus certain projects which would previously have been classified under the 'social' category could now be classified as 'economic' and therefore be included within this increasingly important category.

In addition, these guidelines also gave advice on the use of IAP funds for pump-priming and seed-corn capital which helped determine the city council's use of such funding for projects. One project, for example, which was classified (and funded by the DoE) as an economic project, was described in the IAP Submission Document as a 'dance hall with associated training facilities for 400'. This was a bid put forward on behalf of the Afro-Caribbean community to convert a large building into a dance hall and social centre, and to provide workshops for young people to develop skills in musical equipment repair, etc. However, it was seen by all concerned in the city council as a recreational project, and indeed its project officer was from the Recreation and Arts Department. When asked why this was classified as an economic project, the project officer replied that as it had a bar, it was bound to make money!

Secondly, the DoE guidelines on the preferred capital/revenue split of the programme influenced project selection. By the 1982/3 programme it was made clear that an overall split of two-thirds capital spending to one-third revenue spending over the whole IAP was to be aimed for. This made capital projects even more attractive, given that the overall programme was being increasingly silted up with social projects which had a high revenue element. Site assembly/factory unit bids, which were comprised almost entirely of capital expenditure, became favoured projects in the economic category of the IAP, regardless of their relative merit, against projects with a greater revenue element. Such capital-based projects, incidentally, are also the ones most likely to be statutory rather than from the voluntary sector and to be the more 'traditional' sort of economic projects rather than innovative ones.

Over the five-year period 1979/80 to 1983/4, projects involving site assembly and/or factory unit provision accounted for 55 per cent of the total city council expenditure on the economic aspect of the IAP. In some cases, more than £1 million could be spent on a single project of this type, for example, developing a large old factory into smaller, modernized units. Such schemes are the traditional concerns of the Estates Department, and the vast majority could not be considered innovative or experimental; indeed many were speculative and have been profitable. Of the factory units constructed, most have been let at commerical rents, with the rent and rate relief scheme being applicable only to certain enterprises according to strict criteria. The IAP was, then, hardly the source of radical economic regeneration of the inner city.

Finally, the success of each authority's IAP, at least before the introduction of the UPMI in 1985, has been judged by the DoE almost exclusively on the basis of their spending performances rather than with any concern for effectiveness. The IAP operates on an annual cycle with an absolute cut-off at the end of each financial year, so that underspending cannot, except under special circumstances, be carried forward. Underspending, never popular with politicians, was given new emphasis by the DoE as one of the key performance indicators by which an authority's IAP was judged and which, in turn, influences the size of the following year's IAP allocations. Leicester City Council has regularly included a great range of small projects from the voluntary sector which tend to have a large revenue element. Indeed it has typically allocated a greater proportion of its overall IAP funds to the voluntary sector than other programme authorities. Such small,

revenue-heavy projects are, however, often the ones which experience the most difficulty in achieiving 100 per cent spending
performances (for the reasons considered in Chapter 4). This
situation again makes the more traditional statutory and capital-
based projects a very attractive proposition in comparison to
innovative projects. For the economic side of the IAP, this
particularly favours the 'block' bids for large-scale site assembly
or factory unit provision projects as these are not only capital-
oriented but also allow the authority a degree of flexibility in the
programming of expenditure which makes it more likely that full
spending can be achieved.

So it is clear that the DoE's guidelines on the operation of the
IAP have led, in effect, to a bias towards selecting economic
projects which are traditional (site, assembly and factory units
projects, for example), capital rather than revenue oriented, statutory rather than voluntary, and mainstream rather than experimental. The dilemma for the local authority is that with the
increasing strain on main programme budgets for economic
activity, the continuing problems of section 137 expenditure and
the general problem of capital controls imposed by the government upon local authority expenditure, the resources for economic
activity provided through the IAP are becoming more rather than
less important. Nevertheless, with the tightening of the DoE
criteria on expenditure the danger is that local economic activity
is being led by central government guidelines towards an increasingly traditional form of local economic activity.

DoE guidelines are not the only way in which the IAP mechanism tends to frustrate moves to develop a more strategic and
radical local economic and employment policy, however. In
Leicester City Council, the emphasis on the voluntary sector has
led to a particular system of administering the IAP which has had
far-reaching consequences for the bids selected.

Our detailed analysis of the first five years of the IAP in
Leicester showed conclusively how the IAP bid selection process
effectively acted as a free market with bids from both the voluntary and statutory sectors competing against one another for selection by, ultimately, the Urban Programme Sub-Committee (Sills,
Taylor and Golding 1983). This has had two main effects. First,
it has meant that individual projects have been selected on the
basis of their own merit rather than because they met the guidelines and priorities laid down for each year's IAP. Policy has been

determined by the IAP bids selected rather than vice versa: a true case of the tail wagging the dog. The second effect of the open bidding system has been that members are vulnerable to accusations of picking bids in their wards and bargaining with one another to make sure their wards do have some projects selected. To some extent, politics can displace policy, opening the door to pressure, lobbying and patronage. As one very senior officer put it to us, bids can be selected on the basis of 'sleazy patronage' rather than because they will perform the kind of task constructed by working groups and area review bodies set up to determine annual IAP priorities. In the last couple of years there have been moves to prioritize areas of IAP activity *in advance* of receiving bids, but this still has not overcome the basic dilemma of what happens when a good bid from a non-prioritized area competes with a poor proposal from a priority area. Ultimately, bids still have to be selected on individual merit: whether they are likely to succeed; whether they fulfil DoE criteria; and whether they are able to command sufficient political support from council members.

So we have seen that DoE guidelines have had an inordinate influence upon the nature of local economic activity and that the IAP bid selection procedures have led to activity being determined by the *ad hoc* selection of individual projects rather than strategic or policy considerations. But what strategy or policy guidelines exist anyway? It is clear that activity has run far ahead of policy in terms of local economic development work in Leicester, and again the underlying reasons for this are due to the association between the IAP and local economic and employment development.

In the first six years of the IAP there was no single, coherent policy statement which set out the objectives of the IAP for local employment and economic development. Indeed, one of the striking features of the city's policy-making process in this field has been the number of different 'layers' of policy which have been formulated. The Employment Liaison Group, the Economic Topic Group, the Key Issues 1 Working Group, the Employment and Economic Development Unit and the Planning Department have all variously been involved in formulating 'long-term strategic aims', 'main objectives', 'principles' and 'guidelines' relating to economic and employment activity in the city. The relative status of each of these layers of commitment remains unclear and it has thus been difficult to distinguish priorities for action from wider and more long-term aims, such as 'improving the living and working conditions for all of Leicester's citizens' or 'reducing the stigma of unemployment'. The problem of translating such long-term overall aims of local authority economic policy into a coherent set of policies capable of implementation has yet to be finally resolved. A draft strategy document was drawn up by the Employment and Economic Development Unit in mid-1985, but this was only relevant to the work of this one unit, and did not consider the wider aspects of economic development activity being pursued in other sections of the council. Although by mid-1987 attempts were made to coordinate economic-related activity being carried out in all relevant council departments, an employment and economic development strategy had *still* to be adopted by the city council. (It must be said that fragmentation of policy development was not the monopoly of the city council: Leicester-shire County Council, who are also involved in Leicester's IAP, have an economic development unit in the Department of Planning and Transportation and an employment unit based in the Chief Executive's Department).

Local economic *activity* in the meantime has continued to run ahead of policy development, with some new and more radical initiatives being undertaken. such as the establishment of a low pay unit and a welfare benefits campaign by the City Council. Interestingly, the impetus for both these initiatives came through the IAP bidding mechanism, with local voluntary groups involved in poverty work developing the initial proposals, which were subsequently taken over by the city council and funded through main programmes. In addition, there is a new contracts monitoring unit and an increased emphasis on local economic research and in supporting alternative forms of business enterprises such as cooperatives and community businesses. These are precisely the sort of new and innovative initiatives that members like to see developed but they remain uncoordinated with the other, traditional and very high spending elements of economic development activity such as site assembly, infrastructure and factory unit building. Policy analysis and coordination have fallen behind the pursuit of actual projects due to the fragmented responsibilities for carrying out activities in the local economy (Employment and Economic Development Unit in the Chief Executive's Department, Planning Department carrying out research and monitoring of local economic and employment trends, Estates Department involved in site assembly and small factory units, etc.), the lack of corporate structure for formulating and implementing an authority-wide local economic and employment policy, and IAP considerations as outlined above.

Finally, the link between the IAP and the emergence and growth in size and importance of employment and economic development units must be noted. As we have seen, the IAP and its resources gave a new impetus for local economic activity in Leicester. For Leicester City Council's Employment and Economic Development Unit, and Leicestershire County Council's Employment and Economic Development Units, developing and managing IAP-funded projects is an important aspect of their work. The development of large, prestige IAP projects can do no harm at all as these young units strive for credibility and status within their respective local authority structures. Within the voluntary sector in Leicester, the county council has been particularly criticized for favouring large, shiny new factory unit developments over smaller and less visible community-based schemes: 'all the better to show the Minister around'.

In this section we have considered the policy framework within which Leicester's emerging economic and employment strategy has been developed. Three main points have emerged from this analysis. Firstly, the City Council has developed an increasingly interventionist approach to the local economy in response to growing unemployment and job losses; secondly these economic activities have increasingly been constrained and determined by urban programme considerations, principally the DoE's guidelines, and finally, that this growing scale of economic activity has often taken place in a strategic vacuum. We can now go on to examine the actual package of economic projects as they have been implemented and to assess how problems of implementation have further pushed the programme back towards more traditional areas of economic development.

Putting it into practice: implementing IAP economic projects

Implementation is clearly a central concern for all those involved in local economic development activity and the IAP, for there is little value in establishing policy frameworks and selecting programmes of action if these cannot be implemented effectively. The implementation of the economic element of the IAP is, however, fraught with difficulties, not least because the 'problem' to be tackled is so difficult to define. A central problem is that of the 'shifting target': how can a policy be devised to address a problem that is itself rapidly changing in nature and scale? It is debatable whether the dilemmas arise from the problem itself, or the means of attacking it, or both. On the one hand there are conflicting and sometimes contradictory diagnoses of the local economic problem (is it a result of national policies or a peculiarly local phenomenon, is it structural, cyclical or a result of individual pathology, is it a result of too much governmental interference in market forces or not enough?) and on the other hand there is the uncertainty over the nature of intervention which should be used (urban programme, main programme, regional initiatives, central government industrial policy, import controls, etc.) and its scale (what resources are available, how much cash is needed to tackle the problems?). In addition to these uncertainties over the nature of the problem and the most appropriate means of tackling it, there is the added dilemma that the 'problem' itself is constantly being changed by the action of the existing policies. How far has the local economy and labour market today been shaped by the preceding years of deliberate local authority intervention in it through both the IAP and main programmes? What would have happened anyway, in the absence of such interventions?

It is against this background that the question of assessing the impact of policies must be set. If we examine the actual 'package' of economic and employment projects funded between 1979/80 and 1983/4, how far does the overall pattern of activity thus shown match the council's view of the overall direction policy should be taking? If local economic policy is to go beyond the symbolic (something must be seen to be done) and the *ad hoc* (funding projects purely on individual merit rather than being guided by strategic considerations) then effective monitoring and assessment of policy outcomes is necessary.

To begin, we can examine the actual economic and employment projects supported through Leicester's IAP from 1979/80 to 1983/4 (Sills, Taylor and Golding 1986). By April 1984, some £6.3 million worth of economic projects had been supported through the IAP, £2.5 million of these being funded in 1983/4 alone. The IAP then was supporting a very considerable investment in employment and economic projects, and almost seventy separate projects had been approved for support by this time. A wide range of projects had been supported, from site assembly and factory unit provision, which accounted for over 55 per cent of total expenditure on all projects from 1979/80 to 1983/4, to projects helping the unemployed and disadvantaged worker (15.7 per cent), training projects (15.0 per cent), grants/loans and business advice (9.4 per cent) and workshop projects (4.2 per cent). Over the five-year period examined, total expenditure on economic initiatives rose steadily from £696 000 in 1979/80 to £2.5 million in 1983/4, reflecting both the increased concern that action should be taken in the local economy by the council and the increased emphasis placed on the economic aspect of the IAP by the DoE. There was also a significant change in the types of project supported over the period with an increased emphasis on training and projects to help the unemployed, and slightly less reliance on mainstream site assembly/factory unit provision. Nevertheless, the analysis of the IAP economic element shows the disparity between the overall 'package' of economic projects selected in any one year and that actually implemented. Council members, having considered the IAP bids on the table each year, select a group of these to form an overall package. In some years, they have tended to favour a slightly different set of projects, for example, schemes to help the young unemployed or projects aimed at women's needs. However, for a number of reasons, it is frequently the case that the actual package of projects *implemented* in any one year is considerably different to that which was originally selected. The effect of this, yet again, has in every case been to make the actual package of projects implemented more traditional and mainstream than that originally selected. The key factor behind this situation is 'slippage' or underspending.

'Slippage' is the term used to describe the shortfall between actual and planned expenditure. Slippage is a particular problem for the IAP as, unlike other local government activities, the city council is not allowed to carry forward into the following year any resources that have not been spent, with any such money being returned to the DoE. A high slippage figure, then, not only represents an absolute loss of resources to the city council, and to the projects which have underspent, but also means that the IAP package originally approved is significantly distorted.

Slippage can happen for a variety of reasons, such as voluntary projects not being able to find suitable premises and staff for their projects early enough, and thus underspending in their first year; building projects being delayed due to bad weather; and the notorious unreliability of original cost estimates, particularly from voluntary sector bids. Under the IAP mechanism, when it looks likely that a project is going to underspend, resources are switched to projects which are much more likely to be able to spend the money. Typically, this has led to an increase in actual expenditure on the more mainstream and statutory projects, such as block schemes to assemble and clear sites for industrial development or refurbishing older industrial premises. In contrast, slippage has effectively meant that less money has actually been spent on the more innovative and experimental projects, particularly those from the voluntary sector, where there are not full-time officers to set up and 'trouble-shoot' for the project.

Slippage is crucial to the success or failure of the IAP projects. Even if the more radical and innovative projects have made it through the IAP bid selection process, which, as we have already outlined, is biased towards more mainstream, statutory activities, they can still fall at the implementation stage, through slippage. Even if individual projects are successfully implemented, the overall implementation problems tend to increase the relative expenditure on traditional projects which have a track record as 'good spenders' and decrease it on the innovative schemes. So once again, the reliance on the IAP to provide funding for local economic and employment projects is a factor which tends to undermine attempts to move away from traditional and mainstream approaches based on the physical regeneration of the urban economy and towards more innovative schemes, particularly those which have a high revenue element and are from the voluntary sector.

It is worth looking at the main problems of implementation in more detail to show the forces at work. Our research into the operation of the IAP in Leicester over a six-year period showed that a number of voluntary sector economic projects have simply been too large, complex and ambitious to be planned and managed purely on a voluntary basis.

A key problem is that of the financial management of large voluntary projects, particularly those that employ or train substantial numbers of staff. The voluntary sector plays a major role in

Leicester's IAP, and often large and complex projects are approved for funding on the expectation that voluntary management committees will plan, establish and manage such projects to a professional standard. This has frequently proved a very difficult task for voluntary sector representatives who may have plenty of enthusiasm for their project but only limited time and limited skills to properly cost up and establish projects successfully. A number of large, voluntary sector economic projects have had to be taken over by the city council precisely because their sheer scale and complexity proved impossible to manage by a voluntary management committee. It is acknowledged that in several cases, the pressure on members and officers to boost the economic side of the IAP to meet DoE guidelines led to the acceptance into the funding programme of projects which in fact needed a great deal more initial working up: it was these projects which experienced some of the worst difficulties in becoming established.

A second problem is that of voluntary projects being able to properly cost up and assess the feasibility of their proposed schemes. Underestimating the costs of schemes has been a widespread problem for voluntary sector schemes (as well as some statutory ones). This is often due to a lack of knowledge about the likely costs of a project, particularly the purchase of premises, but it may also be due to a misguided attempt to keep projected expenditure levels artificially low in order to have a greater chance of getting a bid into the IAP. Once projects are accepted into the programme and the real work of establishing and running the project begins, under-costing can then become a very serious problem: hence the number of voluntary sector IAP projects which have collapsed altogether or which have had to be taken firmly under the wing of the local authority until they are fully established as viable schemes. In Leicester, our research has shown that a number of voluntary sector local economic projects have needed very intensive support and guidance from local authority officers, both in designing the initial scheme and then in getting it established and running efficiently. Given the need for this support, and the number of problems such projects are likely to face in their establishment, particularly where they employ or train sizeable numbers of people, it is easy to see why large, capital-intensive schemes coming from the statutory sector are, in comparison, an attractive proposition for the local economic sector of the IAP.

A further problem area lies with those economic projects which have a training function supported through the MSC but which have ambitions to become commercially viable. The problems here include the MSC's rules that trainees have to leave the scheme after one year, just as they are acquiring the necessary skills, and also that MSC trainees can only be used to make 'socially useful' goods which are not to be sold commercially for profit. Where a project is attempting to develop a marketable product range and to generate income these restrictions can be serious. Our research raised a number of questions in relation to the use of the MSC-funded workers by projects intending, eventually, to establish themselves as commercial enterprises, and these were subsequently recognized by the city council itself. A main point to emerge was that the fixed 'overheads' budget from the MSC encouraged projects to apply for large numbers of places in order to obtain large overheads budgets. This frequently meant that projects, instead of starting small and growing as demand or productivity rose, found themselves with a large work-force they could not support by commercial activity. Yet another related dilemma is the MSC's instruction that projects should draw trainees from all over the district, yet many voluntary sector training projects were set up specifically in and for one small community only.

The problems of project implementation can hardly be stressed enough. Our analysis of the economic aspect of the IAP in Leicester shows that whilst a huge amount of officer and member time and effort was spent on discussing IAP priorities and objectives and on assessing bids, the attention paid to the *implementation* of the programme was comparatively scant. Project officers interviewed were frankly scathing of the difficulties some of the projects were allowed to get into, usually through poor initial support and advice.

Two points emerge from this. Firstly, it can be questioned whether the voluntary sector is the right place to manage large projects which train and/or employ substantial numbers. Secondly, without due regard to implementation, council members and the community at large find themselves with an *actual* IAP which is much more traditional, statutory, and capital-heavy than the one they first approved to go to the DoE, due to slippage and the need to insert projects which are likely to spend their allocation before 31 March each year. In short, a neglect of the *means* leads to a dilution and distortion of the *ends*.

Conclusion

The past ten years have seen the urban problem being defined increasingly as an economic problem, the root cause of poverty and urban decay being diagnosed as the collapse of the urban local economy. This redefinition of urban policy coincided with an increase in concern by local authorities about their local economies and a period of policy innovation not only by radical Labour authorities but more generally by local authorities in the field of local economic initiatives.

However, as the analysis of this chapter has illustrated, whilst radical economic and employment policies claimed to be a significant departure from local authorities' traditional role within their local economies, in a period of deep recession and the collapse of manufacturing and rising unemployment, their success in reversing decline has frequently been imperceptible. The resources available to a local authority are insignificant in relation to the scale of the problem to be tackled. Further, the lack of resources available has encouraged local authorities to seek funds wherever possible, e.g. the MSC and IAP, and, as the case of Leicester served to illustrate, policy has been shaped as much by the terms and conditions imposed by outside funding bodies (DoE and MSC) as by the policy-makers in the local authority. In addition, Leicester's experience highlights the scale of support necessary if a policy is to be implemented by using third parties outside the organization, e.g. the voluntary sector, in the name of participation and local democracy.

This is not to say that local authorities do not have an important role to play in local economic development. They remain major employers and purchasers and, therefore, wield significant economic power. They can play an important role in bringing together funds from a variety of sources now available for economic development, highlight the needs of particular deprived groups in their area and play an important advocacy role. Nevertheless, if we go beyond the rhetoric of even the most well-resourced, interventionist local authorities, we have to question their claims to be 'restructuring for labour'. Under the appropriate structures, and with sufficient resources, local authorities *would* be well placed to assist in the drive to boost the economy and cut unemployment, not least because of their knowledge of the particular training needs and investment requirements of their local areas. With more resources and increased powers to intervene, supported by central government, local authorities could assert a key role in inner city economic regeneration. Under the present structures, however, local authorities have neither the resources nor the powers to effect significant changes in the local economy, or create substantial numbers of jobs.

In the case of the IAP, it is clear that the gap between the problem to be tackled (in 1987 one in five of Leicester's work-force was unemployed) and the resources available (a total allocation of £5.4 million for the whole of Leicester's IAP in 1987) is so huge that it can only be bridged with reference to our argument in Part One; that the IAP is less a serious attempt to tackle the 'urban problem' than a means to effect 'symbolic reassurance', making sure that something is seen to be done. The IAP is not the only vehicle for such gesture politics in the inner city economies, of course. There has been a stream of central government initiatives on local economic regeneration which bypass local councils – enterprise zones, urban development corporations and, most recently, inner city task forces. Nevertheless, the IAP has a particularly high local political profile, due to its reliance on community consultation and voluntary sector involvement.

Given this situation, the programme is especially open to the criticism that it provides little more than a flurry of well-intentioned and well-publicized local activities, the overall impact of which is minor in comparison to the scale of the problem. Individual projects can be efficient and effective in meeting their own objectives – providing training places, building factory units, creating drop-in centres for the unemployed – but taken as a whole the economic aspect of the IAP cannot hope seriously to challenge inner city industrial decline to any significant degree. The IAP's economic dimension is essentially concerned with working at the margins, but doing this, at least in Leicester's case, in a very visible, very public way. The visibility of the economic side of the programme, together with the increased reliance placed on it by the DoE, has vested IAP economic initiatives with an importance far outweighing their actual significance.

6 The public and the programme

One of the features that the IAP shares with recent poverty programmes is the emphasis it places on public participation. The standard model employed by such programmes is to designate certain areas in the inner city for priority action and to provide a combination of central and local government finance to assist the residents to run special projects for the benefit of their district. The purpose of public involvement is twofold: firstly, to generate and implement new ideas; secondly, to break down the barriers between government and the governed.

The difficulties that such programmes have encountered are now legendary. When President Johnson's War on Poverty was launched in 1964, it called for the 'Maximum Feasible Participation' of residents in the design and management of new projects. However, within a short time the programme had collapsed with what Moynihan (1969) described as 'Maximum Feasible Misunderstanding'. In Britain in 1968, the Community Development Projects, which were set up to encourage self-help initiatives amongst the communities of certain deprived towns, encountered similar problems in attempting to put the concept of public participation into practice, and Home Office funding was rapidly withdrawn.

It could, therefore, be considered surprising that in 1977 a new government initiative launched to tackle urban deprivation should not only contain a commitment to public involvement in the programme but, in the concept of partnership, make it the central feature.

In this chapter we explain why public participation has been both a persistent feature of poverty programmes but also their most persistent problem. We then examine how public participation has been incorporated into the IAP and what effect this has produced.

Public involvement in poverty programmes

There are three main reasons why public participation seems to have secured a permanent place in poverty programmes, despite the enormous problems it seems to produce.

1. *The theory of poverty.* A central feature of the early programmes was an explanation of poverty based on individual pathology. If the principal cause of poverty lay with the poor themselves in terms of their apathy, their personal behaviour and their domestic mismanagement, then the only long-term solution was to work with and on the poor, helping them to help themselves. Closely allied to this perception of the role of self-help was a scepticism as to the role that government should play. Was not welfare sapping the initiative of the poor and bureaucracy just another problem with which they had to contend? The appeal to the grass roots, then as now, was a powerful one that mobilized a whole contextual framework of direct and purposeful action, unfettered by bureaucratic constraints that could change the circumstances of the poor by changing their attitudes. As we shall see, *Policy for the Inner Cities* combined a commitment to self-help and community effort with a recognition that government services were producing alienation amongst some residents.

2. *The need for economy.* A characteristic feature of poverty programmes has been the low level of resources they have been allocated, compared both to other government spending programmes and to the scale of the problems they ostensibly address. The IAP is no exception in this respect for it stressed that no additional resources were available other than through the redirection of main programmes. Clearly the need for economy is a priority but is there not a credibility gap between the resources allocated and the size of the inner city problem? Not if the problem is defined as being small scale and best treated by local self-help schemes. What is required is not massive government intervention but pump-priming resources for special projects.

3. *Symbolic reassurance.* Among the principal advantages of a poverty programme are the political benefits that accrue, permitting a high profile, low cost public demonstration of the government's commitment to tackling the problems of the inner city. This factor goes a long way to explaining the

continued popularity for launching new poverty programmes despite the well-publicized shortcomings, both conceptual and practical, of their predecessors.

As Chapter 4 has argued, a primary function of the state is to attempt to secure the conditions necessary for the accumulation of profit. To do this it seeks to promote social harmony. Poverty programmes offer the state two opportunities:

1. The chance to demonstrate its concern about problems of the inner city to the public at large, reclaiming the inner city from the muggers and the dangerously indolent.
2. The chance to direct assistance to those who are in most need and/or are likely to cause most disruption to social harmony.

Evidence for this hidden agenda for the poverty programmes can be found in both the location and timing of initiatives. Poverty programmes have been concerned almost exclusively with what is called (variously) urban deprivation, where resources are aimed specifically at the ghettos of the large cities. It is significant, for example, that in the IAP initiative, the DoE have insisted that urban deprivation be tackled in the inner city areas of partnership and programme authorities rather than wherever it occurs throughout the authorities. Despite the wealth of evidence that poverty is a large-scale problem that is geographically dispersed, the policy solutions continue to insist that it is concentrated in small pockets within the inner city.

To understand this apparent dilemma, we must consider the state's need to preserve public order. It is the physical concentration of deprivation that exists in the ghetto which is the defining characteristic of urban deprivation. It is this concentration which poses a threat to public order and the legitimacy of the state and makes the urban poor the political priority that the more dispersed suburban or rural poor are not.

A second factor suggesting a legitimating role for poverty programmes is found in the timing of the various initiatives. Thus President Johnson's War on Poverty was launched in 1964 in a direct response to the worst rioting ever witnessed in the United States. At the height of the disturbances, as the ghettos were aflame, there were more Americans being killed on the streets than in the jungles of Vietnam. With America being seen by many as a cultural weather-vane for Britain, fear was keenly felt that growing poverty amongst a rapidly expanding black community would provoke a similar response. In 1968, Enoch Powell delivered his 'Rivers of Blood' speech in which he saw violence as the inevitable outcome of high levels of immigration from the Commonwealth. Three weeks later, Harold Wilson announced the British Urban Programme.

Thus, we argue, it has been for a combination of conceptual, financial and political reasons that successive governments, on both sides of the Atlantic have found it expedient to support special poverty programmes. These programmes have three features: they are small in scale, concentrating on particular locations in the inner city, commit relatively minor amounts of public resources and emphasize the need for self-help and public participation to secure an improvement in the inner city.

The role of the community in the IAP

Whilst the IAP was offering a partnership between government and the people, who was being invited to join and what were they expected to do? *Policy for the Inner Cities* was vague on both counts, opting as usual for a comprehensive rather than analytical approach. Under paragraphs entitled 'Local Communities' and 'Voluntary Bodies' a variety of partners are listed: local people, local residents, voluntary groups and bodies, tenants' and residents' associations, local councils of social service, settlements and charities, and informal groups such as pensioners' clubs, trade unions, chambers of commerce and neighbourhood councils. The reasons why these various groups were invited to join the partnership were similarly wide-ranging:

Involving local people is both a necessary means to the regeneration of the inner areas and an end in its own right. Public authorities need to draw on the ideas of local residents, to discover their priorities and enable them to play a practical part in reviving their areas. Self help is important and so is community effort. (para. 34)

The notion of the IAP harnessing the goodwill and energies of local people is in line with the romantic and nostalgic view of 'community' outlined in Chapter 3: that the IAP could revive the wartime spirit and decent values of the working class enabling them to pull together with the government to fight the problems of urban decay.

However, the portrayal of community in the White Paper is contradictory: on the one hand it celeberates the potential that exists for self-help within inner city communities, yet on the other acknowledges the lack of community spirit as a problem. In its section on social disadvantage the White Paper states that:

There is a collective deprivation in some inner areas which affects all the residents, even though individually the majority of people may have satisfactory homes and worthwhile jobs. It arises from a pervasive sense of decay and neglect which affects the whole area, through the decline in community spirit. . . . All this may make it harder for people to maintain their personal standards and to encourage high standards in their children . . . this collective deprivation amounts to more than the sum of all the individual disadvantages with which people have to contend. (para. 17)

The concept of community has a central role in the partnership established through the IAP to tackle the problems of the inner city, but, as the White Paper acknowledges, the decline in community spirit and the collective deprivation that follows can be a problem in itself. This begs major questions, therefore, about the nature of the role that the community might play.

An examination of both the existence and meaning of 'community' in the inner city was conducted as part of our research in Leicester (Golding and Sills 1983; Sills, Tarpey and Golding 1981). The concept of community was approached from two angles. Firstly, indicators of community activity were constructed from measures of people's behaviour, such as participation in voluntary associations, and secondly, we examined people's perception of their community and locality.

In their classic study *Family and Kinship in East London*, Young and Wilmott (1957) identified stability of population as a key factor in community life. It takes time for newcomers to settle in, get to know people, identify themselves with the area and to develop community responses towards common problems. This can be difficult in areas of high turnover. Within a ten-year period most of the areas surveyed in Leicester had experienced a 50–70 per cent loss of their original populations, with a fifth of the population in the inner area zones changing every two years. Stability and turnover cannot be considered in isolation from residents' preferences. Being unwilling to move is very different from being unable to. In the city council's seven priority zones our survey found that between half and two-thirds of the residents wished to move.

The evidence from the turnover of population does not in itself refute the existence of communities but rather questions whether communities are coincident with localities. This was explored in greater depth by looking at the contact networks of residents within the survey areas. Whilst the majority of people (80 per cent) had family or relatives living in Leicester there was a much weaker link with the specific locality. Thus 84 per cent of residents in one priority zone had family or relatives living in Leicester, yet only a third of these lived within that zone itself. People were asked if they had visited their family, their friends or their neighbours within the last month and the survey found a higher degree of contact with family and friends, the majority of whom lived outside of the area, than with neighbours, who, by definition, lived close by.

In addition to the closest ties in the community, those of family and friendship, the investigation of community considered the wider patterns of contact within the community resulting from people's leisure time activities. Whilst such contact is informal and unstructured, it is a way in which residents can get to know the people who live in their area, and it represents the public face of community involvement as distinct from private sociometry.

Residents were asked to say which of a series of activities they had engaged in within the last month. These activities were wide-ranging, covering indoor and outdoor, active and passive pastimes, and covered a broad age range. The survey found that with the exception of going to the pub in most areas, and going to a place of worship in the predominantly Asian areas, all other activities, such as going to parks, playing or attending sport, etc., attracted a minority of residents, usually less than a third. The survey showed that there were a significant number of people in each area who participated in virtually none of the activities, except visiting or being visited by family or friends. Whilst not necessarily housebound, it was clear that the lives of these people centred around their homes. Amongst this group are the frail and elderly, the sick and the disabled. The need to look after children hindered access to leisure in some families whilst lifestyles were notably home-oriented among the Asian community.

Another measure of the level of community activity was provided by the degree of direct participation by residents to community affairs. Residents were asked if they belonged to organizations, such as tenants' or residents' groups, and if they did, whether they regularly attended their meetings. The results confirm that only a very small proportion of residents are actively involved in community affairs. To explore both the positive and negative aspects of community life, residents were asked, 'Do you think people have got on well together or not?' This was not a question people found easy to answer, nor to elaborate on. There was an ambiguity in some replies with residents saying that they thought that people did get on well together but, when questioned further, often identified social subdivisions within the community. Thus 'we', the elderly/white community, get on well together, but 'they', the newcomers/Asians, are unfriendly, and do not want to mix. People have comparatively low expectations of community life, claiming that they got on well because 'we haven't had any trouble' or 'people keep themselves to themselves', supporting the notion of privatized lifestyles.

When asked what they disliked about living in their area, the largest single complaint concerned other residents in the area, notably vandals and 'problem families'. People were asked whether they thought that local people could do more to improve their area, and there was found to be a marked similarity between the problems people were concerned with and the actions they thought local people could take. The three main things people thought should be done by their neighbours were to keep the area clean, improve their gardens and houses and control their children.

These all relate to the way a person conducts his or her life and are aimed at reducing the public nuisance caused by irresponsible private conduct. It is significant that comparatively few people interpreted this question in its more positive sense of people either helping their neighbours or in becoming more active in local affairs.

The somewhat romanticized myth of the community as an organic source of energy for the revitalization of the inner city is embedded deeply in the 1977 White Paper. Where absent, this communal lifeblood is seen to have been temporarily diluted by planning blight, family decline or demoralization. Yet, as our survey findings suggest, for residents of many areas of urban poverty, the ties of locality and neighbourhood are frail and tenuous. Ambition, leisure and pleasure centre on home and family, while the plethora of community facilities are but patchily used, and other residents are perceived as a problem as much as a resource. In seeking partnership with 'the community' the IAP was not merely chasing a chimera, it was neglecting a host of problems elided by the happy neglect of the rampant divisions and privatized lifestyle in the areas targeted by the IAP. (Golding and Sills 1983).

Policy for the Inner Cities acknowledges the problem of alienation from government and suggests a partnership between government and public as a solution. This, however, raises questions about the reasons for this alienation and about the adequacy of a partnership through the IAP to tackle them. The research carried out in Leicester confirms that this feeling of alienation is widespread, but casts doubts on the notion that there is a 'community' with whom a partnership can be formed.

Tackling deprivation: from self-help to community action

Having questioned both the concepts of community and partnership, it is worth examining what role the two might be expected to play in reviving the inner city. This role is itself dependent on the nature of the problem to be addressed, which means returning to the conceptual weakness of the White Paper – what is the nature of the inner city problem?

Given the variety of interpretations as to the causes of deprivation, it follows that there is an equally broad range of alternative cures, each demanding a different contribution from the public. Evidence from previous poverty programmes suggests that there are three separate ways in which the public have become involved: through developing self-help (relating to the culture of poverty/cycle of deprivation); extending welfare pluralism (rectifying institutional malfunctioning/maldistribution of resources); and stimulating community action (to combat structural class inequality). Each of these is associated with different theories of deprivation and reflects a very different perspective on the problems of the inner city, and, as such, is aimed at a very different political solution. By examining the different objectives of these various types of voluntary action, we see the opportunities and limitations of each and provide a context in which to assess the comparatively narrow range of partnership options currently on offer through the IAP.

The role of self-help

The form of partnership developed most frequently through the poverty programmes has been self-help, whereby local people are encouraged, through a combination of public money and professional leadership, to effect an improvement in their own situation. This was the original objective for the CDPs before their workers redefined their brief in terms of community action.

The case for developing self-help as a means of tackling the problems of the inner city rests on three arguments:

The ideology of individualism

Central to the philosophy of self-help is the view that individuals are personally responsible for their own welfare and for its improvement. Just as the Protestant ethic preached that thrift and hard work would find their reward both in heaven and on earth, their opposite, vice, was primarily responsible for the condition of poverty. If poverty is seen as the result of sin, then the only lasting solution must come through personal salvation. No amount of charity can help until the individual has abandoned his feckless practices. Welfare merely subsidizes idleness.

More liberal interpretations of poverty prevalent in the twentieth century have emphasized the importance of structural factors (such as unemployment and low pay) as the root causes of poverty and were instrumental in establishing the system of social insurance embodied in the Welfare State. Paradoxically, the failure of the Welfare State to eliminate poverty has been taken by some as evidence of the social pathology of those deviant groups who persist in their rejection of those opportunities offered to improve themselves.

The recent economic decline has witnessed a massive increase in the scale of poverty in Britain. Whilst *Policy for the Inner Cities* chose to concentrate on these economic problems as being the principal issues facing the inner city, it still had concern for the problems of social pathology. This was seen as a 'collective deprivation' arising from a 'pervasive sense of decay and neglect' which is responsible for a 'decline in community spirit' that makes it 'harder for people to maintain their personal standards' (para. 17). The answer is seen to lie in self-help and community effort (para. 34).

Scepticism of state intervention

Closely associated with the ideology of self-reliance is a scepticism as to the value of state intervention. The point can be argued from two standpoints. Firstly, that state welfare can have a negative effect by reducing the incentive to work and sapping individual initiative. Indeed, one of Mrs Thatcher's principal justifications for public expenditure cuts has been that her government has been elected 'to lead people away from debilitating dependence on the State' (*Guardian*, 21 May 1984). To combat a supposed inducement to idleness, welfare schemes have always contained a 'less eligibility' principle to ensure that people claiming benefit had an incentive to seek employment. Secondly, it is argued that state activity is both inefficient and restricting as it operates through an inflexible bureaucracy that is a brake to innovative action. This can be contrasted with the advantages of mutual aid, which is seen to provide the opportunity for a speedy, flexible and sensitive response to local problems.

Financial advantages

Whilst there are arguments to be made for the merits of individual as opposed to state intervention, the current revival of interest in self-help owes as much to the advantages of reduced costs as to any perceived benefits in quality of outcome. It is the policy of the present government to reverse the trend of increasing public expenditure in favour of private services. One of the major ways of reducing the level of state involvement is by transferring the burden of responsibility for care back onto the community or the family. In such a strategy, voluntary action has a major part to play, as Patrick Jenkin, the then Secretary of State for the Environment, acknowledged in 1980: 'When economies have to be made we are right to look to the voluntary sector to take on a larger share of what has to be done' (*Hansard*, 31 March 1980, col. 48). A policy to encourage self help can thus appeal to a broad range of factors favoured by a Conservative philosophy: a belief in individual action, a scepticism of the benefits of state intervention and a desire to reduce the burden of public expenditure.

The encouragement of self-help was one of the stated aims for inner city partnership in the White Paper. Evidence from previous poverty programmes, however, suggested that the scope of its contribution would be limited. The role of self-help in tackling urban deprivation had been widely criticized from a theoretical standpoint by the CDPs (Higgins *et al*. 1983).

The CDP teams argued that a solution to poverty which is based upon self-help assumes that individuals are primarily responsible for their problems. If the real causes of poverty lie with society rather than the individual then self-help appears to be blaming the victim for his or her own poverty, and merely tries to cope with the consequences. By aiming to help people adapt to their situation it supports the status quo and may dissuade people from taking more appropriate action. The shortcomings of the self-help strategy have been set out by John Benington, who was leader of the Coventry CDP. In common with other CDPs, the Coventry project soon encountered difficulties in attempting to apply the Home Office's 'self-help' brief to the problems facing the residents of Hillfields in Coventry:

The most obvious blatant problems that people experienced were not internal and pathological but external. They arose from the very low incomes people were having to live on and the very poor housing and environment in the district. These problems were not peculiar to that neighbourhood; they were the same as the problems which were afflicting large sections of the working class population throughout Coventry. (Benington 1975, p. 175)

Given the limitations of a self help strategy, the principle justification for such a policy is seen to lie more in its financial expendiency. With the notable failure of self-help poverty programmes on both sides of the Atlantic, it is difficult to see how, despite the rhetoric, much can be expected through this form of partnership.

The case for welfare pluralism

The principal partnership activity of the IAP has been the funding of voluntary sector projects. These projects aim to extend the range of non-statutory service provision and collectively represent a commitment to welfare pluralism. Each year, partnership and programme authorities invite the voluntary sector to submit requests for funding, then select from these schemes a limited number to be included in an IAP Submission Document. As this has now become the standard model for IAP partnership, it is easy to forget what is being included and excluded from this option. Supporting projects from voluntary groups implies a particular form of partnership with a particular type of partner.

The welfare pluralism of the IAP can be seen as part of a development which has seen a massive rise in the number and range of voluntary organizations over the past thirty years. These have arisen partly as service providers, filling gaps left by the Welfare State, and partly as pressure groups that can campaign for change in statutory provision. At the same time there has been a marked increase in the level of state support for the voluntary sector in recent years. In its report, *The Future of Voluntary Organisation* (1978), the Wolfenden Committee estimated the level of central government support for the voluntary sector in 1976/7 as £35.4 million. This has risen to £290 million in 1983/4, according to figures published by the National Council for Voluntary Services.

The case for expanding and supporting the voluntary sector was set out by the Wolfenden Committee who saw the two principle contributions that could be made by voluntary organizations as 'the strengthening of collective action in meeting important social needs and the maintenance of a pluralistic pattern of institutions' (p. 21). Whether stated explicitly or merely implied, these have been the major justifications for the state support of voluntary organizations, and will be examined in turn below:

Collective action

There are three ways in which voluntary organizations can help meet social needs. Firstly, they can help extend the scope of existing provision. Voluntary organizations can attract new resources, both in terms of finance and manpower, that can provide services in addition to current statutory provision. The Wolfenden Committee estimated that the work done by volunteers was equivalent to that of 400 000 full-time staff. Voluntary organizations do not just provide duplicates of statutory services, for, it is argued, with their independence and flexibility they perform an innovative role that can develop new approaches to secure provision. Secondly, voluntary organizations can help improve the quality of existing statutory provision. This can come about either through the work of pressure group campaigning for changes in government services, or through direct competition, where it is argued that the loss of statutory monopoly can increase consumer choice. Thirdly, voluntary organizations can introduce new services which may have received a low priority from the public sector. Thus much of the recent developments in counselling and advice services have come about through the activities of voluntary organizations.

Pluralism

The Wolfenden Committee argued that the contribution of the voluntary sector extended beyond the provision of services *per se* to include the educational benefits accruing to a pluralist society in teaching people participatory skills:

Over and above the direct contribution of the voluntary system in meeting social needs, we must also consider the case made for its contribution to the pluralistic character of our political and social institutions. The principal benefits attributed to the voluntary sectors in this sense relate mainly to its potential as a means of enabling widespread direct public participation. In the modern industrial state, dominated by large-scale political, economic and social institutions, most people have little opportunity to shape the society in which they live. The voluntary sector offers the possibility of direct involvement. In the space between the loosely structured informal system and the more strictly organised statutory system, people can use the medium of the voluntary organisation to join with others in devising means to meet their own needs, or those of others they wish to help. In consequence, those involved will not only feel less alienated from the society in which they live, but they will also be engaged in altering its nature both directly through the activities they undertake and, less directly, through the signals sent by these activities to the statutory system on the nature of shifts in public interests. In the process, those participating in the voluntary system often acquire experience and skills that enhance their capacity to contribute in roles they fill in other sectors of society. (p. 29)

The pluralist advantages of participation were recognized in

Policy for the Inner Cities. Having recognized that in some areas people feel 'alienated from or apathetic to the impersonal workings of central government and local government too', the answer was seen to lie in greater participation by local people, seen as an end in its own right. What sort of partnership is being offered through the support of voluntary sector projects and what does it hope to achieve?

Firstly, in this invitation to partnership, the IAP is appealing primarily to the organized public, those who are actively involved in voluntary groups. As we have seen from the consideration of community participation, this is a comparatively small number of people. Secondly, the bidding for, and allocation of, IAP resources implies a particular form of partnership which seems to encourage pluralist service provision that can supplement, complement or extend existing statutory provision. This partnership seeks to tackle the problems of the inner city by changing the distribution of resources. In terms of theories of deprivation, welfare pluralism attempts to make its contribution through its ability to target resources through services to disadvantaged communities. It does not seek to change the distribution of power, nor does it pose a threat to the manner in which decisions are taken by the local authority. What the IAP partnership offers in practice is new services and facilities (workshops, drop-in centres, brick-cleaning schemes) which are addressed to particular 'inner city' problems. To a greater or lesser extent they offer the organizers the opportunity to be a partner with the local authority in the management of *that project*. What is clearly not on offer is a wider partnership that extends beyond the projects funded by what is only a marginal activity for the local authority.

Partnership in the IAP has, in practice, meant little more than the funding of voluntary sector projects. As a way of tackling the problems of the inner city, this has been criticized from a variety of angles. The conservative case against welfare pluralism rests on the related issues of efficiency, cost and accountability. Alarm is expressed that the rising cost of providing permanent subsidy to the voluntary sector was merely a hidden expansion of the Welfare State.

In an economic climate in which rigorous attempts are being made to cut back public support for non-productive (i.e. non-wealth-producing) activities the £290 million of government money going to the voluntary sector in 1983/4 is wasted, just as if it had gone to the statutory social services. Secondly, there is concern that the attempts to increase the professionalism and organization of the voluntary sector may produce exactly the same problems of inefficiency associated with bureaucracy that are alleged to occur with public provision. If the justification for supporting the voluntary sector is that it can avoid the top-heavy bureaucracy found in government services there is a danger that this support may be self-defeating. Finally, the efficiency of voluntary organizations is questioned. Do they have the expertise to manage public funds? This point was expressed forcefully by one chief officer in Leicester:

'Some of these voluntary set ups are a front, as it were, of 2 or 3 people who are a management committee, but when you come to look at them they are only people who said they'd do it for a short time, so there's no continuity and often no motiviation. . . . I wonder with some of the voluntary projects how strong their management committees are to take on these quite big responsibilities. . . . You can't take on employing people lightly these days. You've got to have a proper treasurer, and proper management policy and a job description. Are these voluntary bodies properly constituted? I sometimes wonder whether all this money that is so hardly got and so hardly won is going into voluntary bodies which are not very strong. Also there is the danger of channelling money into criminal hands because who vets these committees? There isn't that control. There is a lot of public money going in and there is not that much control.' (Sills, Taylor and Golding 1983, vol. 2, p. 43)

The pluralistic objectives of partnership as pursued through various poverty programmes can also be questioned. If the poor are apathetic and do not get involved in politics, their voices will be unheard. In such circumstances, special programmes are required that will draw the poor into the political arena and encourage them to participate. This, in essence, was the strategy behind the 'maximum feasible participation' clause in the American poverty programme. However, as Dearlove (1974) comments, 'It is one thing to argue that the absence of public participation and influence by the poor is deplorable, but it is quite another to say that participation is the solution to the problem of poverty' (p. 37).

Seen from a structuralist perspective, poverty is the outcome of economic and political powerlessness. The poor are poor because they lack power when they bargain for resources, either through the labour market or in the political arena. 'Apathy and defeatism are natural responses to a situation of powerlessness' (Dearlove, p. 38). Participation is only the answer if apathy and alienation are the problem. There have been plenty of well-publicized examples over the last twenty years of redevelopment schemes where the voice of the community concerned has been anything but silent but where their political power was insufficient to win their case. Again, to quote Benington's experience in Coventry,

It became clear that local people did not see more communication leading to better solutions to their problems at all. On the contrary, they were in direct dispute with the authorities about the nature of their needs and their aspirations. They saw the problem as their difficulty in influencing decisions which affected their lives in the directions which they wanted. It was not a consensual situation. It was a situation where residents believed they had a different interest from that represented by the public authorities. Communication was there in plenty; communication that was only sometimes vocal or articulate, expressed mostly in informal social settings, but sometimes through the traditional means of petitions and public meetings and at times of exceptional frustration even in minor acts of insurrection. (Benington 1975, p. 176)

The radical case against pluralism is that the imbalance of power in society creates a 'mobility of bias' in the political system. 'The flaw in the pluralist heaven is that the heavenly chorus sings with a strong upper class accent' (Schattschneider 1960).

Stimulating community action

The final form of voluntary activity promoted through poverty programmes is community action. In both the United States, in the War on Poverty, and Britain, through the CDPs, attempts were made to organize local communities to fight for resources and power.

Community action is about organizing protest and strengthening the political bargaining position of disadvantaged groups and communities. It takes as its premise the structuralist view of poverty as being endemic in a capitalist society. In such a view, the state exists to service the needs of capital and, whilst forced to respond to demands placed upon it from powerful interests, such as organized capital or labour, it can afford, by and large, to ignore the interests of the poor. In such circumstances, where the government's definition of needs and priorities is seen to ignore those of disadvantaged position, the only solution is to increase the bargaining strength of these groups through community action.

Community action in the IAP is notable by its absence, despite the fact that it was the model adopted by local workers in the early poverty programmes on both sides of the Atlantic. In both cases an examination of the difficulties facing local residents in deprived districts concluded that the state itself was one of the major problems. Instead of developing suitable projects, like support groups for alcoholics, local workers organized marches to the town hall! This was clearly the 'unacceptable face of the voluntary sector' and has never been permitted to make an appearance in the IAP. Whilst strongly championed in previous poverty programmes why was community action never permitted on the partnership agenda for the IAP? The answer lies in the uncomfortable experience of community action eminating from previous poverty programmes. In the United States, and then in Britain, both politicians and administrators questioned spending public money in organizing protests against itself. As such, community action had first surprised then annoyed the people whose power it threatened, as witnessed by the experiences of Mayor Richard J. Daley in Chicago:

In the second fiscal year of the anti-poverty program, beginning July 1, 1965, community action received 45 per cent of the total appropriation, altogether $685 million. But by the spring of that year, protests from city governments about the tactics of the new community action agencies were already pouring in. The issue was policymaking. Mayor Richard J. Daley of Chicago was known to be mightily upset. In the correct tradition of urban, Democratic, ethnic politics, the Chicago anti-poverty program was roaring ahead, and predictably became a champion grabber and distributor of anti-poverty funds. The party was looking after the people. What was not distributed, however, was the power to make such allocations. Do that and one day you wake up and there is no machine. Mayor Daley wanted the poor to be employed *by* the program. *He* wanted to make the decisions about it. (Moynihan 1969, pp. 144–5)

The *raison d'être* of community action is to provide an alternative political voice, because existing political channels fail to reflect the views of disadvantaged groups adequately. On the other hand, given the political inactivity of the poor, community activists will be, by definition, atypical, and it is easy to see how politicians may be sceptical of the true measure of support that exists for this alternative voice from the community. One way of giving legitimacy to community politics is through the creation of alternative political structures, such as neighbourhood councils. Whilst this idea was hinted at in *Policy for the Inner Cities* (para. 35), it has clear implications for the distribution of political power and has not been adopted.

Finally, community action can be seen as another instrument of coercion, providing the state with information about local problems and local activists, whilst it incorporates and diffuses protest. 'What emerges is a form of community socio-therapy which transforms actions into compliance, reduces community disorganization and integrates marginal groups into the established order' (Dearlove 1974, p. 33).

The effect of trying to organize groups in a formal way can create tensions that work against the spontaneity of protest and is self-defeating. Governments are used to dismissing protest that comes from an 'unacceptable' direction. When the protest is made acceptable it loses its impact and is incorporated. Again, to quote from the American experience:

In North Carolina, especially in Durham, 'community action with special emphasis on participation organization has . . . channelled dissatisfaction and unrest into forms and issues which can be dealt with' (Strange 1969, p. 29).

Peter Bachrach, making the same point for Baltimore, places great stress on the morale-building effects of federally funded programs, which

provided black groups essential sources of power and conflict and decision-making arenas in which the struggle for power could be fought out in the open and *within the confines of the political system.* (Moynihan 1969, p. 274)

As community action is not considered by the DoE to be an acceptable form of partnership, it has not been developed through the IAP. The main interest in considering its absence is the indication it gives about the limitations to partnerships and the motivations of governments that implement them. The rejection by the DoE of projects with even a mild hint of community participation about them suggest that the government is interested in harnessing through the IAP the advantages of small-scale poverty programmes (low cost, high profile) without incurring the heavy disadvantages associated with the community action element of previous programmes.

Table 9 *Differing explanations of urban problems*

Theoretical model of problem	Explanation of the problem	Location of the problem	Key concept	Type of change aimed for	Method of change
Culture of poverty	Problems arising from the internal pathology of deviant	In the internal dynamics of deviant groups	Poverty	Better adjusted and less deviant people	Social education and social work treatment of groups
Cycle of deprivation	Problems arising from individual psychological handicaps and inadequacies transmitted from one generation to the next	In the relationships between individuals, families and groups	Deprivation	More integrated self-supporting families	Compensatory social work, support and self-help
Institutional malfunctioning	Problems arising from failures of planning, management or administration	In the relationship between the 'disadvantaged' and the bureaucracy	Disadvantage	More total and coordinated approaches by the bureaucracy	Rational social planning
Maldistribution of resources and opportunities	Problems arising from an inequitable distribution of resources	Relationship between the underprivileged and the formal political machine	Underprivilege	Reallocation of resources	Positive discrimination policies

Structural class conflict	Problems arising from the divisions necessary to maintain an economic system based on private profit	Relationship between the working class and the political and economic structure	Inequality	Redistribution of power and control	Changes in political consciousness and organization

Source: Bennington (1975)

We have seen in this chapter that various models for public participation in poverty programmes have been developed arising from implicit theories about the causes of urban deprivation. The contradictions involved are well illustrated by the spectacular collapse of both the War on Poverty in the United States and the CDP initiatives in Britain, when differences in both the interpretation of deprivation and the role of the public in poverty programmes emerged between the state and local activists.

That public participation surfaced in the IAP initiative testifies to the strong financial and political imperatives for its inclusion. To ensure that such participation was developed within strict limits the notion of partnership was kept so vague as to be virtually meaningless whilst the mechanics of the IAP kept a tight rein on how any partnership might evolve. With community action kept firmly off the agenda and self-help out of favour as a means of tackling urban deprivation this ensured that welfare pluralism was the main model for inner city partnership. Thus partnership was to be achieved through the funding of short-term projects, which required the approval of both local and central governments.

In the remainder of this chapter we examine what partnership has meant in practice, drawing on our research in Leicester.

Public involvement in Leicester's IAP

There are two reasons why Leicester makes a particularly interesting case study. Firstly, in comparison with other large metropolitan cities, Leicester had comparatively little organized or radical grass roots community activity before the IAP. The majority of tenants' and residents' associations, for example, had been set up on the initiative of the city council to act as liaison groups, rather than by the residents to act as pressure groups. This meant that in Leicester the IAP was starting from scratch and did not, as in some more militant areas, immediately get incorporated into the existing framework of community politics. In such circumstances the IAP could not fail to have an immediate and visible impact.

Secondly, Leicester City Council is widely held to be the programme authority that has done most for the voluntary sector through the IAP, both in terms of involvement in the decision-making process and in the allocation of resources to voluntary groups. Taken as a model of good practice the Leicester experience is revealing of both the opportunities and limitations of partnership.

In common with most other local authorities, Leicester City Council did not have any formal mechanism for public consultation, other than through the electoral process. In line with the traditional model of local government, services were provided by officers of the council under the direction of elected members, who were in turn accountable to the public through the ballot box. The problems of apathy and alienation encountered by this relationship were a prime consideration for the IAP.

Through its call for partnership, the IAP was making the case for consultation to bridge the alleged gap that had grown between the government and the governed. However, whilst hinting at the opportunities afforded by area management schemes and neighbourhood councils, *Policy for the Inner Cities* offered no advice on how local authorities should structure their partnerships with the public. The only formal requirement was that local authorities should give details of their consultative procedures in their IAP Submission Documents. Thus, on this subject, as on so many others, the White Paper offered a statement of intention, but with no clear idea as to how it could be achieved.

The first year of the IAP, 1978, witnessed a hectic debate on the meaning and practicalities of partnership. As local authorities sought guidance from ministers and civil servants, it rapidly became clear that, behind the stalling about tight timetables and the need for a full debate in future, there were no answers.

In the event, when the future came it was under a Conservative government, who brought a very different set of priorities for the inner city. In place of the Labour government's partnership came the strategy of economic revival through market forces, in which the principal form of consultation was to be with the private sector. As public expenditure cuts deepened, and the freedom for local initiatives was constrained, the 'partnership' between central and local government became an open war, as witnessed in rate-capping and the abolition of the GLC and metropolitan counties. In such circumstances it is understandable that the IAP was relegated in importance and its concept of partnership abandoned, at the national level at least.

However, a crucial element of partnership was to be that between local authorities and their public. In the remainder of this chapter we examine how this partnership was developed in Leicester.

In October 1978, when the first round of IAPs had been submitted, the National Council for Social Services (NCSS) undertook a review of community involvement in the inner city programmes. Voluntary organizations in each of the seven partnership authorities and fifteen programme authorities were asked to examine the level of impact of public involvement in the IAP in their area. Of these twenty-two authorities NCSS collected information on eighteen. Despite the obvious limitations of such data, it does provide one of the few opportunities for a comparative assessment of the early partnership activities in the IAP.

The survey found that Leicester was one of only six authorities to have held a series of public meetings in connection with the IAP and one of only three authorities where a voluntary representative had been invited on to an officers' coordinating group. The survey found that in thirteen areas the comments of voluntary organizations were thought to have affected the description of problems and proposals in the IAP; 'only in the case of Leicester was there evidence of more than a minimal importance in these aspects of the programme'. This conclusion says as much about the lack of voluntary involvement in other areas as it does about the situation in Leicester.

Partnership was given a boost by Leicester City Council's policy of supporting the voluntary sector. Whilst figures from the NCVO suggest that most IAP authorities allocate between 10 and 25 per cent of their IAP resources to the voluntary sector, Leicester allocated approximately a third of its IAP to voluntary groups in the first seven years of the programme (*Inner City Areas*, NVCO, July 1983). During this period, there has been a growing interest in the IAP by the voluntary sector in Leicester, and a total of 754 separate bids have been received, of which 193 were approved at a total value of £10.885 million (Table 10).

Whilst the level of resources available through the IAP is out of scale with the problems of the inner city, they are large enough to have made a significant difference to local groups in Leicester. Essentially partnership in the IAP has been pushed through the bidding process and we examine this in two ways: firstly, looking at the involvement of different types of groups in the IAP and the resources allocated to them, and secondly, by examining the experiences of different groups, both of receiving resources and

Table 10 *Allocation to voluntary groups through Leicester's IAP 1979/80 to 1985/6*

	Allocation (£000s)	%	Bids submitted	%	Bids approved
Residents' groups	912.2	8	100	13	26
Religious groups	170.3	2	54	7	7
Urban aid/IAP projects	2429.8	22	179	24	53
National voluntary groups	949.6	9	65	9	16
Leicester voluntary groups (city-wide)	2996.0	28	163	22	42
Local voluntary groups	2841.6	26	160	21	42
Other	585.8	5	33	4	7
Total allocation	10885.3	100	754	100	193

managing projects and also in being 'rejected partners' when their applications were refused.

Due to the variety of voluntary groups seeking IAP funding it was necessary to devise a classification system that could be applied within the limitations of the only comprehensive data source, the standardized information provided by voluntary groups in support of their IAP bid applications. The classification was based on the three principal factors that determined how a voluntary group responded to the IAP:

1. *Resources*. Whilst some groups have premises and full-time professional staff, others have neither and their members meet all costs of preparing and submitting a proposal.
2. *Expertise*. The level of expertise within a group will be an important factor in determining how the group becomes involved in the IAP and, crucially, their dependence on external advice.
3. *Organization*. If a voluntary group has its own support services for appointing staff/paying bills, it can easily handle the administrative demands of a new IAP project. Also if the IAP bid from such a group is turned down it can carry on with its existing activities. However, for the group with no such back-up services an IAP bid will present a number of administrative problems, which may change the character of the group, whilst a rejected bid may lead to the collapse of the group itself.

As we shall see, these three factors operate together to influence the partnership relationship between a voluntary group and the local authority. On the basis of the differing levels of resources, expertise and degree of organisation, we categorized voluntary groups submitting projects to Leicester's IAP into seven groups: (1) residents and tenants associations; (2) religious groups; (3) existing IAP projects; (4) national voluntary organisations; (5) Leicester-based voluntary organisations (city-wide); (6) local voluntary groups, and (7) others (Table 9). The involvement of each will be considered in turn.

1. *Residents' groups.* A distinct category within the voluntary sector contains the many residents' groups who have become involved in the IAP. The majority of residents' groups in Leicester have been set up by the Housing Department to perform a liaison function between the city council and the public, particularly with regard to the Revenue Strategy Programme. As such they have a close relationship with the council and local field workers. Between 1979/80 and 1985/6 residents' groups submitted 100 bids to the IAP, of which 26 were approved at a combined cost of £912 200, being 8 per cent of the voluntary sector's total allocation.

   Residents' groups have opted for a particular form of partnership with the local authority. Two-thirds of their approved projects (seventeen) were for environmental works, supplementing or extending the city council's environmental programmes in many action areas. There are two possible interpretations of such a partnership: one which saw local residents working closely with council officers to improve the environment in their area and another which saw council officers as being the dominant partner, suggesting schemes to residents' groups which they could submit through the IAP.

2. *Religious groups.* A second distinctive subgroup applying for partnership are churches and temples which have a number of characteristics differentiating them from other groups. Firstly, they have a specific religious function which exists outside of any activities they wish to pursue through the IAP. Most of these groups have been established for many years and have a degree of permanence that is in sharp contrast to the ephemeral character of many other voluntary groups. Religious groups

also tend to have their own premises and to serve a specific locality.

Between 1979/80 and 1985/6, religious groups submitted fifty-four bids to the IAP, of which seven (13 per cent) were approved at a cost of £170 300, being 2 per cent of the voluntary sector's total allocation. The majority of bids received were for the repair or improvement of religious buildings on the grounds that they were/or were going to be for community, as distinct from religious purposes. This was an argument for partnership that Leicester City Council rejected in most cases.

3. *Existing IAP projects.* Another important subsection within the voluntary sector is existing IAP and urban aid-sponsored projects. Those groups share three features: a unique funding arrangement, a more detailed knowledge of the IAP and, by necessity, an existing close relationship with their sponsoring authority. Between 1979/80 and 1985/6 existing IAP projects submitted 179 bids to the IAP, the largest of any section of the voluntary sector. Of these 53 (30 per cent) were approved, which was again the highest success rate for any part of the voluntary sector. These projects had a combined value of £2 429 800, being 22 per cent of the voluntary sector's total allocation.

As the IAP has developed in Leicester, more groups are becoming IAP funded, so the influence of IAP projects is expanding. Thus in the first three years of the IAP, existing projects submitted 42 additional bids, compared with 137 in the subsequent four years of the programme. Bids were submitted for three main reasons: to intensify an existing IAP service by employing extra workers etc., to extend the range of work of the project, enabling it to develop into new areas, and finally to clarify the funding arrangements of the existing project. Whilst the first two reasons fall under the category of welfare pluralism, enabling projects to develop the range of services offered, the third reason is an interesting commentary on partnership, that the only way a project feels it can clarify its future funding is to make a formal request through the IAP.

There are a number of explanations for the high activity rate amongst existing IAP projects. To submit an IAP bid requires knowledge (to identify the IAP as a source of funding), initiative (to think of a suitable project), confidence (to apply for funding) and skill (in completing the bid form and negotiating with the council). As existing IAP projects, these groups will clearly have demonstrated their ability on all these counts to have obtained their original support and, therefore, are at an advantage over other voluntary groups when it comes to applying for further funding.

Again, the implications for partnership are not clear. Is support for IAP projects an extension of existing arrangements, building on the partnership already created with the voluntary sector, or is it merely extending the professional voluntary sector? Clearly it represents a professional form of partnership, based on proven success and known expertise, and there is an obvious attraction in funding projects with a good track record. However, this 'safe' partnership with an established group is but one form of partnership and does not necessarily coincide too closely with the image mobilized in the original White Paper.

4. *National voluntary groups*. There are many national organizations with a local branch in Leicester. Between 1979/80 and 1985/6 these groups submitted sixty-five bids to the IAP, of which sixteen (25 per cent) were approved at a combined value of £949 600. With both knowledge of the IAP and organizational expertise these groups were well placed to submit bids in the early days of the IAP when other less well informed groups were still learning about the opportunities available. However, in recent years, the involvement of national groups in Leicester's IAP has declined sharply. Those groups that have participated have tended to be client-based, offering support to a wide range of people. Thus seventeen of the bids received were concerned with health issues with the elderly or the disabled, a further thirteen with children or young people and nineteen with other client groups, such as the poor and single parent families. Collectively, these represented two-thirds of the bids from national voluntary groups.

5. *Leicester voluntary groups*. A large number of IAP bids from the voluntary sector were submitted by Leicester voluntary groups. These were groups which are based in Leicester and organized on a city-wide basis. Collectively, they submitted 163 bids to the IAP, of which 42 (26 per cent) were approved at a value of £2 996 000. Here the variety of projects is matched only by the variety of organizations classified as belonging to the voluntary sector. Thus a number of bids have been made

by institutions, such as Leicester Polytechnic, from housing associations and from umbrella organizations, such as Leicester Council for Voluntary Service.

One of the most interesting features is the size of some projects with qualified staff and high revenue costs. Such projects, like a law centre, demonstrate the willingness of the city council to support expensive schemes, provided they are convinced of the need and of the credibility of the group submitting the proposal. The professional nature of these groups can be seen not only in the thorough IAP applications they submit but also in the professional status of many of the individuals involved, their management committees filled with lawyers and university lecturers.

This 'professional partnership' has seen the development of a range of non-statutory services, such as the Community Press and Community Transport schemes, and particularly in the field of advice initiatives. This level of support provides evidence of the city council's commitment to the voluntary sector and its willingness to experiment with the IAP. However, as we have seen in the discussion on welfare pluralism, this is only one form of partnership. Whilst it is probable that a number of the projects aim to foster self-help and possible that a few aim to stimulate community action, the majority of projects are seen to be concerned with extending the range of services or facilities available.

6. *Local voluntary groups.* These are community-based groups who draw their membership from a specific area and whose activities are centred on or around that locality. Between 1979/80 and 1985/6 these groups submitted 160 bids to the IAP of which 42 (26 per cent) were approved at a value of £2 481 600. It is this partnership with community or local groups that conforms most closely with the ideas contained in *Policy for the Inner Cities* of harnessing the efforts and energies of local people to combat the problems of urban deprivation. But what size and what sort of partnership has evolved?

It is significant that even for an authority committed to funding local groups only a quarter of its allocation to the voluntary sector, and less than a tenth of its total IAP resources, have gone to this type of group. Partly, this is the result of the bidding process. Local authorities can only select from the bids available and in the early days of the IAP community groups lacked the knowledge of the IAP necessary to make a submission. In the first three years of the IAP, local groups submitted only 33 bids compared with 127 in the following four years. Thus the city council's policy of funding local groups has been frustrated in part by its dependence on the IAP bid process.

Whilst the type of bids submitted varied enormously, two-thirds were requests for the provision of facilities and/or staff to enable a group to start up or develop its activities. The principle issue that these bids were concerned with was recreational activities, which accounted for twenty-six (62 per cent) of the approved projects.

Clearly the partnership here was a narrowly based one, with the city council identifying certain issues, such as play or cultural and recreational facilities for ethnic minority groups, as being 'inner area' issues, being best dealt with outside of the programme activities of the local authority.

7. *Other voluntary bids*. Between 1979/80 and 1985/6 thirty-three projects were submitted by groups or individuals that could not be classified under one of the six headings above. Of these bids, seven (21 per cent) were approved at a value of £585 000, all of which were economic projects, conforming to the Government Guidelines for the IAP.

In Leicester, then, the development of partnership through the IAP has been between Leicester City Council and voluntary groups, defined as any organization submitting bids from outside the local authority. The partnership developed has seen the IAP being used to sponsor the development of a range of non-statutory services. This partnership can be of two kinds: a 'professional partnership' with national charities or Leicester groups, or 'community partnership' with locally based groups.

In the former, the local authority is backing the professional expertise of the organization involved to develop a new type of service, whilst in the latter it is willing to delegate one of its own responsibilities to a local group: environmental improvements for residents' groups or cultural and recreational facilities for ethnic minorities, for example.

Finally, this has been a restricted partnership: one that has centred on projects. So far this has not gone beyond the support and management of projects to influence wider relationships between the council, its services and its public.

The experience of partnership

To examine partnership through an analysis of the groups, their projects and their finance is to see but part of the partnership. It is also necessary to consider the experiences of these groups who have been drawn into partnership, firstly, by looking at the experiences of the three-quarters of the bids which never get funded and, secondly, by examining what funding has meant in practice for those groups which have been supported through the IAP. These questions and issues were addressed through a series of interviews with the sponsors of a sample of 227 (30 per cent) of the total 753 projects submitted to Leicester's IAP between 1979/80 and 1985/6.

For most groups, the decision to submit an IAP bid was taken by a small group of people, usually a steering group or management committee. The relationship between this committee and its membership varied between groups, with some claiming that they were in touch with the opinions of their membership whilst others admitted that they were only as representative as the people who attended. Where voluntary groups employed their own workers, then it was often the latter that took the initiatives with the IAP. As one admitted, 'I presented the ideas to the management committee and at the next meeting I presented the bids. At the next meeting I said one has been turned down and at the next one I said they'd all been turned down.'

In practice the offer of partnership is taken up by comparatively few people. The problem with attempting to use projects as a vehicle for developing partnership is that most of the public experience voluntary projects as consumers of a service rather than as partners in the project. The IAP's offer of partnership, therefore, tends to be narrow rather than broad, but one which, as we shall see, has a considerable impact on those who heed its call!

The enormous variation in knowledge, confidence and expertise that exists between different types of groups was reflected in their experience of the bidding process. Professional groups identified the IAP as an opportunity and could detail their staff to draw up estimates, prepare bids, and negotiate with the council. By contrast, smaller voluntary groups were usually told about the IAP, commonly by a sympathetic council worker, on whom great reliance was placed in preparing the bid. Whilst groups formed an alliance with 'their' worker, who was often identified as being 'one of us', the bids submitted showed evidence of a more manipulative relationship. Thus one residents' association claimed to have submitted its bid 'to help the City Engineer' while another group denied all knowledge of their IAP application, which, on further investigation, had been designed and submitted by an over-enthusiastic community worker.

This raises an important dilemma for the concept of IAP partnership as it is the very groups the IAP is meant to help which find the most difficulty in coping with the considerable bureaucracy involved in making an IAP application. The support of project officers in Leicester has been a mixed success with some officers using community groups as a way of securing departmental objectives.

For community groups, the partnership game is played for higher stakes. All the necessary preparatory work involved in submitting a bid is done in their spare time and all costs are met out of their own pockets. Pensioners are not in a position to use the office telephone/photocopier etc. Again the wisdom of using the IAP bidding process as a means of developing partnership is questioned by the obscurity of the exercise to many groups. Whilst professional groups claimed, in general, to have understood the process and to have completed their bid form with ease, the situation for the community groups was very different. There was considerable evidence to suggest that the IAP process itself actually *increased* the alienation between the authority and the public by raising expectations which were never realized. The frustrations felt by many groups were well summed up by one person's experience of the IAP bid form:

'To me as a layman, it made no sense whatsoever. I can read it but I can't understand it. They ask you 'what will it do?' then 'what will it achieve?', then 'what will it benefit?' It's all the same . . . and the finance, God Almighty, how the hell do I know! Surely the finance comes after the bid is approved? . . . You've got revenues, salaries etc. How can you gauge all that if you've never done anything like this before. It is absolutely confusing.'

Given the government's insistence on keeping a tight financial control over the IAP, it is difficult for local authorities to be more flexible in their approach to the voluntary sector. However, if the degree of detail required from the voluntary sector is beyond the ability of many groups to provide, then the extent to which partnership goals can be pursued through the IAP is constrained by the gap between the financial and political acumen of community groups and the administrative demands of a tightly supervised programme.

The survey found a confusion about the IAP process that was endemic, even amongst those groups that were IAP funded. Again, much of the blame rests with basic design faults of the IAP, whereby a programme is put together by one level of government for detailed approval by another. The single question of 'has my bid been approved?' rarely receives a simple reply. The government have added to this confusion with their guidelines dividing IAP expenditure by capital/revenue and economic/social/environmental categories. No longer are voluntary groups concerned with submitting bids to meet needs, they must have a detailed and acute appreciation of IAP bidding tactics and procedures.

To the confusion surrounding the IAP is added the anger of the 75 per cent of groups whose projects are refused – the fractured partnership. Whilst many groups claimed that they were actively encouraged to make IAP submissions, they contrasted the advice and support they received whilst preparing their bid with the bald letter of rejection. In particular, the lack of any reason for rejection was a particular cause of complaint:

'You can never find out why We were very angry. If there was any specific reason why you could avoid the pitfall. I mean, who decides? Is it officers or councillors?'

Rather than reducing the level of alienation in the inner city, the survey found considerable evidence that the IAP was producing some negative effects. For some groups, the distribution of IAP resources highlighted the lack of an inner city consensus, the absence of a single community with a common purpose. Thus tensions existed between white and black groups, each complaining that the other's share of the IAP was too high, whilst the IAP also exposed conflicts between generations, by giving facilities to young people that their elders disapproved of.

Finally, the veil of mystery surrounding the IAP bidding process and the allocation of resources generated considerable hostility in some quarters towards the city council. In the absence of a detailed understanding of the complexities of both policy and bureaucratic constraints the actions of the city council were interpreted, in crude terms, as vote catching.

The impact on a group of having its bid rejected could be serious. At one level it could involve loss of face by the bids promoters:

'We are figures of fun . . . we look like burkes and it's the city council that have made us look like burkes.'

As a result a number of people who were previously active in the community withdrew from an involvement in local affairs.

'All we want is to be left alone.'

Again this questions whether a bidding process is the most effective way of attempting to secure an inner city partnership. Secondly, a rejected IAP bid can cause a collapse in support for local groups.

'For us the Inner Area Programme has been negative, focusing discontent, opened sores and caused trouble. . . . It has been a problem for the (Tenants') Association. People are disinterested and are going away. They think we're not doing anything.'

The IAP is a partnership but between whom? We have seen that the public has not got involved in the IAP, but experience the IAP as consumers of its services. The partnership created through the IAP has been between three groups of people, each with their own set of interests: the local authority, project management committees and project workers.

As the local authority is responsible to the DoE for the IAP and the allocation of resources it has a duty to ensure that money is being spent correctly. However, at what level and in what degree of detail should an authority attempt to supervise voluntary sector projects? In practice projects recorded very different experiences of this supervision. On the one hand some groups complained of excessive interference from their project officer whilst on the other hand some groups claimed they never saw their project officer. The principal conflicts surrounded those areas of local authority activities which are under-professionalized (like recreation) where officers felt most threatened by voluntary groups. These tensions have been heightened by the changing resource position in the IAP, which has resulted in much stiffer monitoring and review procedures. No longer can projects be assured of a continuing partnership.

Summary

Public participation performs an essential part in the attempts by a poverty programme to break down the barriers between the government and the governed. It is assumed that creating greater opportunities for the latter to get involved in the former will help reduce the alienation and apathy of inner city communities. However, beneath the rhetoric of participation and partnership there is a process of:

Incorporation: strangling dissidents and community protest by red tape and failure.

Marginalisation: transferring statutory functions and responsibilities onto voluntary groups.

Divisiveness: the bidding system reinforces inequalities in resource distribution leading to political alienation increased by rising but frustrated expectations and the ever real threat posed by the withdrawal of grant aid to projects.

A further attraction of partnership for poverty programmes is the opportunities offered for a populist devolution of power or, as a minimum, the chance to target resources directly to key groups. However, this freedom is all to easily diverted into a cynical use of funds for political patronage targeting resources to key opinion leaders or groups rather than to the needs of the communities they claim to represent.

As we have seen, poverty programmes, despite their failures, have a seemingly irresistible appeal for governments, both central and local. The euphoria of partnership was well encapsulated in one document published by Leicester City Council which invited IAP bids from the voluntary sector under the title 'Have a Go'. This chapter has explored what the reality of the IAP lottery has meant to the groups which have attempted to join in partnership with the city council in Leicester. We have seen that beneath the innocence of partnership rhetoric there exists a darker reality.

Many community groups who 'Have a Go' may be less than enthusiastic about the usefulness of completed bidding forms, published annually by the city council, to the police. As one officer commented, 'They (the bid forms) are marvellous. They tell us who is active, in what areas and what they're up to. We know who belongs to which groups and what they're trying to do.' Perhaps community policing is in every sense a form of partnership but not one in which all voluntary groups would actively wish to be engaged.

7 Conclusions

The urban problem has been a pressing issue for governments ever since industrialization concentrated the poor in appalling conditions in rapidly growing cities, creating the potential for violent disturbance and disorder. Attempts to contain and control the urban problem have ranged from workhouse relief to sending in the dragoons. In this book we have been concerned with one recent approach, the poverty programme, which in one form or other has been used extensively by governments on both sides of the Atlantic in response to recurrent spasms of unrest.

All such programmes have been rich in rhetoric, none more so than the IAP with which this book is concerned. This was described by Peter Shore, Secretary of State for the Environment, at its inception as the programme to 'reverse the engines of decline' in the inner city. Now that the inner city is once again back at the top of the government's agenda, and the rhetoric of concern is in full flood, it is useful to examine exactly where the engines of exodus of the latest initiative have taken us. By looking in detail at the experience of one city, where there has been a genuine local commitment to tackle the problems of urban decay, we have seen how each of the IAP's central features, be it partnership, innovation, redirection of main programmes or economic renewal all have failed to halt, let alone reverse, the engines of decline in the urban living conditions of many of Leicester's poorest inhabitants.

The attraction of poverty programmes of this kind is their ability to offer a high profile, low cost legitimation exercise for governments unwilling to face up to the resource implications involved in really tackling urban deprivation. To succeed, a poverty programme must bridge the credibility gap between the magnitude of its vision and the paucity of its resources. Can programmes such as we have described here ever succeed?

There are no simple lessons to be learnt from our analysis of one stretch in the long history of attacks on the scourge of urban poverty in Britain. Two clear themes do emerge, however. First the scale of urban poverty continues to dwarf and outrun the level of urban programmes by a factor which calls into real doubt the extent to which these programmes are seriously intended to tackle the roots of the problem. After all, to take one simple but telling piece of data, in 1985/6 no less than 17.2 per cent of average household expenditure in the East Midlands region was derived directly from social security payments (*Employment Gazette* 1987, p. 490). The likely impact and knock-on effect of more generous benefits can only tempt speculation. But with this level of penetration and significance in the local economy by transfer payments through the social security system it is obvious that even marginal shifts in the level of benefits are bound to have major economic and social consequences of a kind as yet beyond most urban poverty programmes. Second, time and time again we can see the use of urban policy to bypass institutions of local political action and create tighter ties between the state and local communities.

In the wake of the recession in the early 1980s and the monetarist experiments of the first two Thatcher administrations the gulf between the poor and the better off had become immense. By 1983 over 16 million people were living in or on the margins of poverty – 31 per cent of the population, an increase of 47 per cent since 1979. This increase was particularly large for the population below pension age. In a city like Leicester the growing gap was stark. According to one analysis, by 1983 over 68 000 people in Leicester, 31 per cent of the population, were managing on incomes of less than 140 per cent of supplementary benefit levels, a 42 per cent increase since 1979. Even for many of those in work the prospects are often bleak. Over 51 000 workers were earning below the Council of Europe low pay threshold in 1985 and unemployment in what had been a boom economy in the first twenty years after the war had risen to a level above the national average, with 45 per cent of the city's unemployed out of work for over a year, and more than ten unemployed people for every notified vacancy. While the IAP has redirected additional resources to the city these have been overshadowed by much larger cuts imposed on public expenditure, particularly those made in the Housing Investment Programme.

In such a context it would be simple to conclude that urban policies are no more than what we have described in Chapter 3 as symbolic reassurance. Certainly this is a major function. But the second feature of such programmes, whose scale is far from negligible (£3.5 billion in the Urban Programme alone between 1979 and 1987), and whose real achievements should not lightly be dismissed, is the avenue they have offered for increasing central control over local policy implementation. Classically poverty programmes, representing high profile responses to acute symptoms of distress, have always appealed over the head of local institutions directly to the 'people'; they articulate a corporatist populism which dismembers structures of poverty and inequality into the more manageable mechanics of urban administration.

This attempt to bypass local government has become an explicit purpose of the urban policies of the Thatcher governments. As we have seen in Chapters 3 and 4, controls over local discretion in the management of initiatives like the IAP have become increasingly detailed and extensive. By 1987, with local government reform high on the agenda, Lord Young, the Trade and Industry Secretary, declared that he wanted to 'appeal directly to the people living in the inner cities'. The Environment Minister, David Trippler, was more explicit about the political motivation when he promised at a conference on inner city funding that the government 'intended to sweep away the obstacles to development' including 'incompetent or downright loony councils' who stood in the way (*Guardian*, 1 July 1987).

One means of negotiating this bypass has been the increasing use of the private sector in the partnership between government and community, and in part this reflects the limits to municipal enterprise we have explored in Chapter 5. The other is directly political, using fiscal measures to reduce the available funding for local government from central government, and most recently in the introduction of the community charge, or poll tax. The establishment of a uniform business rate, assessed centrally, will immediately increase the proportion of local money controlled directly from Whitehall from under 50 per cent to about 75 per cent. The aim is, among other things, ostensibly to make local authorities more accountable by making them more susceptible to a wider range of local residents, more of whom become liable to the charge. 'Effective local accountability must be the cornerstone of successful local government. . . . The burden of rates is carried on too few shoulders' creating a 'mismatch between those who are entitled to vote in local elections, those who benefit from local authority services, and those who pay domestic rates' (*Paying for Local Government*, Cmnd 9714, 1986, pp. vii–5). In other words it is the urban poor who are benefiting from services and it is they who should pay. As Oppenheim (1988) has pointed out, this achieves a subtle shift in which accountability ceases to mean of the government to the voter in the polling booth, but of the service consumer to the government through the ability to pay. As an aspect of policy for the urban poor this takes us firmly back to victim blaming in a form of outstanding fiscal ingenuity.

If our analysis shows a marked drift to centralization on the one hand, and minimalization of urban programmes in the face of growing inner city poverty on the other, what are the particular issues raised by the implementation of an initiative like the IAP?

The IAP began with high ideals of innovation, participation and coordination in inner city policy, involving inner area residents in the improvement of their social, economic and physical environment. The IAP was to be a source of new ideas and a method of levering main programmes towards tackling urban deprivation. However, as we showed in Chapter 4, it is clear that at every stage of the planning cycle of the IAP there have been major difficulties which have in turn tended to frustrate these ideals. The chapter showed that the IAP has now been reduced to little more than an annual resource allocation, with all pretence of 'bending' main programmes being dropped.

The disparity between the aims and outcomes of the programme was also examined in Chapter 5, with particular reference to its economic aspect. The 'urban problem' has been defined increasingly as an economic problem, with the root cause of urban decay being diagnosed as the collapse of the urban local economy. The DoE has been pushing local authorities to put more emphasis on the economic side of the programme by spending a higher proportion of their IAP allocation on economic projects, and especially on capital expenditure. The effects of this, combined with other pressures (most notably those on section 137 expenditure) have tended to frustrate the radical ambitions of local economic activity, and reinforced the bias towards funding more traditional projects rather than new and innovative schemes. In examining the limits to municipal socialism, the IAP must be considered a significant brake on attempts to 'restructure for labour'. Given the gap between the resources available and the scale of the problem to be tackled, the book questions whether the economic aspect of the IAP is much more than a well-intentioned but nevertheless marginal exercise in the politics of the visible – ensuring something is *seen* to be done.

The relationship between the voluntary and statutory sectors is another key issue examined in detail in the book. The IAP has always contained a strong rhetoric of public participation, and in Leicester as in many other areas the entire programme has been based around getting as many people and voluntary groups as possible to put in bids to be considered for IAP funding. However, as Chapter 6 showed, beneath the surface of these notions of participation and the devolution of power lies a rather different experience. The IAP's 'open-bidding' system was shown to lead to the incorporation and marginalization of many voluntary and community groups participating in the programme, and further, to divisiveness as the more informed and well-connected groups succeeded in getting their bids accepted in comparison to less articulate and knowledgeable groups. The outcome of this has not only been a growing cynicism amongst community and voluntary groups but also a markedly unequal pattern of IAP resource distribution across the priority zones.

The IAP was introduced, as we have outlined earlier, in response not only to the specific issue of urban deprivation but also to wider concerns of race and social disorder. The findings of our research question whether the programme has successfully addressed either of these issues. Since 1979, Leicester (in line with several other urban areas) has experienced inner city riots twice, in 1981 and 1983. Black groups have certainly benefited from the programme in terms of funding for their projects, but the basic racial inequalities remain in the city: the IAP has not been able to reduce the high relative level of ethnic minority unemployment or the poor housing conditions of many black families. In the absence of bending main programmes, the IAP remains a marginal, low cost programme which could not hope to alter the structural inequalities between the ethnic groups in the inner city.

The urban programme in its many guises remains a touchstone of major partisan differences. In part this is a question of whose inner city the programme is for. While some sing the praises of urban development corporation initiatives in places like the

London Docklands, others bemoan the arrival of chic super-expensive penthouses on reclaimed inner city land. Nicholas Ridley, the Secretary of State for the Environment after the 1987 election, argued that the inner cities offered insufficient executive housing. 'It is no good having only rows and rows of council houses and tower blocks. An American executive doesn't want to live in a council house somewhere at the back of Manchester.' Told, erroneously, that there were no golf courses in the north-east he suggested, 'There has bloody well got to be a golf course. There ain't no room for prejudice.' He meant against the Japanese businessmen for whom he felt that such services would be an investment incentive (*Guardian*, 19 June 1987).

These partisan differences are more general, however. In the drift to Thatcherism the thesis is clear.

The public-sector dominated municipal solutions of the past simply have not worked. They have made things worse because they were based on a misunderstanding of what makes cities – and other areas – successful. We should draw a line under them. Cities grew and flourished because of private enterprise and civic pride; it is private enterprise, backed by helpful, direct, and concentrated government action, that will renew them. (Patten 1987, p. 8)

For others however:

The government's entire programme is based on the false premise that all the problems of the inner city are the fault of local government. . . . The programme is about rolling back the functions of local authorities and channelling public money – which could have been used to build and repair council homes, regenerate public works, and provide better school facilities – into the pockets of the speculator and private landlord. (Blunkett and Hodge 1987, p. 7)

These divergencies underline the root of programmes like the Inner Area Programme in underlying values. In the last decade these values have reflected the more general drift towards a reshaping of the normative basis of public policy in a radical individualism based on self-help, selectivity, and privatisation (see Golding, 1983). That these programmes are essentially political and ideological rather than simply technical is the key to understanding their failings. Authors like Marris and Rein (1967) and Moynihan (1969) have previously analysed the inadequacy of urban poverty programmes to match their own rhetoric. The sheer scale and structural mechanics of urban poverty are so entrenched in the social and economic fabric of our society that it is clearly unrealistic to expect the dabbling of recurrent bouts of administrative virtuosity seriously to address the issues. In this context an initiative like the Inner Area Programme is best understood as a redefinition rather than as a solution to the drastic and endemic problems of poverty and deprivation faced by large numbers of residents of Britain's inner cities. Those problems will not be solved until they are given a new language and a new perspective outside the inadequate mechanics of urban policy alone.

Bibliography

Allnutt, D. and Gelardi, A. (1979) 'Inner Cities in England', *Social Trends*, vol. 10, pp. 39–51.

Archbishop of Canterbury's Commission on Urban Priority Areas, (1985) *Faith in the City: A Call For Action By Church and Nation*, London, Church House Publishing.

Benington, J. (1975) 'The flaw in the pluralist heaven: changing strategies in the Coventry CDP', in Coventry Community Development Project, *Final Report*.

Blunkett, D. and Hodge, M. (1987) statement quoted in *Guardian*, 26 June 1987, p. 7.

Boddy, M. (1984) 'Local economic and employment strategies', in M. Boddy and C. Fudge (eds), *Local Socialism*, Macmillan.

Brown, M. and Madge, N. (1982) *Despite the Welfare State*, SSRC/DHSS Studies in Disadvantage, Heinemann Educational Books.

Centre for Local Economic Strategies (1986) *Local Work* No. 1.

Child, D. and Paddon, M. (1984) 'Sheffield: steelyard blues', *Marxism Today*, vol. 28, no. 7, pp. 18–22.

Cochrane, A. (1985) 'The attack on local government: what it is and what it isn't', *Critical Social Policy*, vol. 12, p. 44–62.

Cochrane, C. (1983) 'Local economic policies: trying to drain the ocean with a teaspoon', in J. Anderson, S. Duncan and R. Hudson, *Redundant Spaces in Cities and Regions? Studies in Industrial Decline and Social Change*, Academic Press.

Committee of Public Accounts (1985/6) *Tenth Report: The Urban Programme*, House of Commons Paper 81.

Davies, T. (1980) *Inner Cities, Building Bridges: Linking Economic Regeneration to Inner City Employment Problems*, University of Bristol, School for Advanced Urban Studies.

Dearlove, J. (1974) 'The control of change and the regulation of community action', in D. Jones and M. Mayo (eds) *Community Work One*, Routledge & Kegan Paul.

Department of the Environment (1977a) 'Local Government and the Industrial Strategy' (Circular 71/77).

Department of the Environment (1977b) *Press Release* No. 835.

Department of the Environment (1981) Inner Area Programme Guidelines, DoE, July.

Department of the Environment (1983) *Urban Deprivation*, Information Note No. 2, Inner Cities Directorate.

Duncan, S. and Goodwin, M. (1985) 'The local state and local economic policy: why the fuss?' *Policy and Politics*, vol. 13, no. 3, pp. 227–53.

Dunleavy, P. (1979) 'The urban basis of political alignment', *British Journal of Political Science*, vol. 9, no. 4, pp. 409–43.

Dunleavy, P. (1980) *Urban Political Analysis*, Macmillan.

Dunleavy, P. and Husbands, C. (1985) *British Democracy at the Crossroads*, George Allen & Unwin.

Economist, 23 November 1985, p. 36.

Edelman, M. (1977) *Political Language: Words that Succeed and Policies that Fail*, New York, Academic Press.

Edwards, J. and Batley, R. (1978) *the Politics of Positive Discrimination*, Tavistock Publications.

Employment Gazette (1986) 'Patterns of Household Spending in 1985', December, pp. 485–91.

Engels, F. (1969, orig. 1845) *The Conditions of the Working Class in England*, Panther Books.

English, J. (1979) 'Access and deprivation in local authority housing', in C. Jones (ed.) *Urban Deprivation and the Inner City*, Croom Helm.

Eyles, J. (1979) 'Area-based policies for the inner city: context, problems and prospects', in D. T. Herbert and D. M. Smith (eds), *Social Problems and the City: Geographical Perspectives*, Oxford University Press.

Flynn, R. (1986) 'Urban politics, the local state and consumption problems in recent social and political theory', in Goldsmith and Villadsen (1986).

Friedland, R. (1982) *Power and Crisis in the City: Corporations, Unions and Urban Policy*, Macmillan.

Friedland, R., Fox, R., Piven, F. and Alford, R. (1977) 'Political conflict, urban structure and the fiscal crisis', *International Journal of Urban and Regional Research*, vol. 1, no. 3, pp. 447–51.

Gaunt, R. (1982) 'Economic development by district councils', *Initiatives*, November.

Gladstone, F. (1979) *Voluntary Action in a Changing World*, NCVO.

Golding, P. (1983) 'Rethinking Common Sense about Social Policy', in D. Bull and P. Wilding (eds), *Thatcherism and the Poor*, Child Poverty Action Group, pp. 7–12.

Golding P. and Middleton, S. (1982) *Images of Welfare: Press and Public Attitudes to Poverty*, Oxford. Martin Robertson.

Golding, P. and Sills, A. F. (1983) 'Community against itself: social communications in the urban community', *Journal of Community Work and Communication*, vol. 20, December, pp. 177–93.

Goldsmith, M. and Villadsen, S. (eds) (1986) *Urban Political Theory and the Management of Fiscal Stress*, Gower.

Goodwin, M. and Duncan, S. (1986) 'The local state and local economic policy: political mobilization or economic regeneration', *Capital and Class*, vol. 27, Winter, pp. 14–36.

Gough, I. (1979) *The Political Economy of Welfare*, Macmillan.

Greater London Council (1985) *The London Industrial Strategy*.

Guardian, 29 July 1987, p. 1.

Gulley, E. (1926) *Joseph Chamberlain and English Social Politics*, New York, Columbia University Press.

Hall, S., Critcher, C., Jefferson, T., Clarke, J. and Roberts, B. (1978) *Policing the Crisis*, Macmillan.

Harrington, M. (1962) *The Other America: Poverty in The United States*, New York, Macmillan.

Harrison, M. L. (1986) 'Consumption and urban theory: an alternative approach based on the social division of welfare', *International Journal of Urban and Regional Research*, vol. 10, no. 2, pp. 232–42.

Higgins, J. *et al.* (1983) *Government and Urban Poverty*, Oxford, Basil Blackwell.

Hills, J. (1987) 'What happened to spending on the welfare state?', in A. Walker (ed.), *The Growing Divide*, Child Poverty Action Group.

HM Chief Inspector of Constabulary (1987) *Report 1986*, House of Commons Paper 32.

Hogget, P. (1987) 'Local government, not bureaucratic but Byzantine', *Local Work*, No. 5, pp. 14–15.

Holtermann, S. (1976) 'Areas of urban deprivation in Great Britain: an analysis of 1971 census data', *Social Trends*, No. 6, HMSO.

Home Office (1969) Press release – *Gilding the Ghetto*, 16 July.

House of Commons (1973) 'Debate on social problems', 1 November, cc. 340–1.

House of Commons (1977) *Policy for the Inner Cities*, Cmnd 6845, HMSO.

Jarman, B. (1983) 'Identification of underprivileged areas', *British Medical Journal*, vol. 286, pp. 1705–9.

Jarman, B. (1984) 'Underprivileged areas: validation and distribution of scores', *British Medical Journal*, vol. 289, pp. 1587–92.

Lawless, P. (1981) *Britain's Inner Cities: Problems and Policies*, Harper & Row.

Leach, S. and Stewart, J. (1983) *Approaches in Public Policy*, George Allen & Unwin.

Leicester City Council (1978) *Leicester Inner Area Programme 1979–82: Submission Document*.

Leicester Mercury, 29 June 1987, p. 12.

Mackintosh, M. and Wainwright, H. (1987) *A Taste of Power: The Politics of Local Economics*, Verso.

McGregor, A. (1979) 'Area externalities and urban unemployment', in C. Jones (ed.), *Urban Deprivation and The Inner City*, Croom Helm.

Marris, P. and Rein, M. (1967) *Dilemmas of Social Reform*, Penguin.

Marshall, M. and Mawson, J. (1984) *Local Economic Initiatives Sutdy*, vol. 1, Centre for Urban and Regional Studies, University of Birmingham.

Massey, D. (1978) 'Regionalism: some current issues', *Capital and Class*, vol. 6, pp. 106–25.

Massey, D. (1982) 'Enterprise zones: a political issue', *International Journal of Urban and Regional Research*, vol. 6, no. 3, pp. 429–34.

Milner Holland Report (1965) *Report of the Committee on Housing in Greater London*, Cmnd 2605, HMSO.

Mollenkopf, J. H. (1983) *The Contested City*, Princeton University Press.

Moore, B. and Rhodes, J. (1979) 'The impact of regional policy', Social Sciences – Political Economy and Taxation (D 323, Block 2, Unit 7), Open University Press.

Moynihan, D. P. (1969) *Maximum Feasible Misunderstanding*, New York, Arkville Press.

O'Connor, J. (1973) *Fiscal Crisis of the State*, St Martins Press.

Oppenheim, C. (1988) *A Tax on All the People: The Poll Tax*, Child Poverty Action Group.

Page, E. (1986) 'Fiscal pressure and central–local relations in Britain', in Goldsmith and Villadsen (1986).

Pall Mall Gazette, 11 February 1886.

Paterson, J. T. (1981) *The Welfare State in America, 1930–1980*, British Association for American Studies.

Patten, J. (1987) 'Inner city big bang', *Guardian*, 17 April.

Piven, F. and Cloward, R. (1972) *Regulating the Poor: The Function of Public Welfare*, Tavistock Publications.

Plowden Report (1967) *Children and Their Primary Schools*, Report of the Central Advisory Committee on Education, HMSO.

Rees, G. and Lambert, J. (1985) *Cities in Crisis: The Political Economy of Urban Development in Post-War Britain*, Edward Arnold.

Robinson, R. (1986) 'Restructuring the Welfare State: an analysis of public expenditure, 1979/80–1984/85', *Journal of Social Policy*, vol. 15, no. 1, pp. 1–21.

Roger Tym and Partners (1981/2) *Monitoring the Enterprise Zones*, Year 1 and Year 2 Reports.

Saunders, P. (1981) *Social Theory and The Urban Question*, Hutchinson.

Sears, D. and McConahay, J. E. (1973) *The Politics of Violence*, Boston, Houghton Mifflin.

176   *The Politics of the Urban Crisis*

Seebohm Report (1968) *Report of the Committee on Local Authority and Allied Personal Social Services*, Cmnd 3703, HMSO.

Shutt, J. (1984) 'Tory enterprise zones and the Labour movement', *Capital and Class*, vol. 23, pp. 19–44.

Sills, A. F., Tarpey, M. and Golding, P. (1981) *Inner Area Research Project: Social Survey First Report*, Centre for Mass Communications Research, Leicester University.

Sills, A. F., Tarpey, M. and Golding, P. (1982) *Asians in the Inner City*, Centre for Mass Communications Research, Leicester University.

Sills, A. F., Taylor, G. and Golding P. (1982) *Housing and the Inner City*, Centre for Mass Communications Research, Leicester University.

Sills, A., Taylor, G. and Golding, P. (1983a) *Policy for the Inner City?*, vol. 1, Centre for Mass Communication Research, Leicester University.

Sills, A. F., Taylor, G. and Golding P. (1983b) *Policy for the Inner City?*, vol. 2, Centre for Mass Communications Research, Leicester University.

Sills, A. F., Taylor, G. and Golding, P. (1986) *The Inner Area Programme and Local Economic Development*, Centre for Mass Communications Research, Leicester University.

Smith, S. (1883) 'Social Reform', *The Nineteenth Century*, vol. 75, May, pp. 896–912.

Spencer, K. M. (1975) *Comprehensive Community Programmes*, Institute of Local Government Studies.

Stedman Jones, G. (1976) *Outcast London: A Study in the Relationship between Classes in Victorian Society*, Peregrine Books.

Stewart, M. (1987) 'Ten years of urban policy', *Local Link*, January, pp. 6–11.

Stewart, M. and Underwood, J. (1983) 'New relationships in the inner city', in K. Young and C. Mason (eds) *Urban Economic Development: New Roles and Relationships*, Macmillan.

Storey, D. (ed.) (1985) *Small Firms in Regional Economic Development in Britain, Ireland and the United States*, Cambridge University Press.

Sullivan, D. (1987) 'Indigestion and the radish', *The Chartist*, May/June.

Townsend, P. (1979) *Poverty in the United Kingdom: A Survey of Household Resources and Standards of Living*, Penguin.

Townsend, P. (1987) *Poverty and Labour in London*, Low Pay Unit.

Ward, J. and Williams, P. (1986) 'The government and local accountability since Layfield', *Local Government Studies*, Jan./Feb., pp. 21–32.

Ward, M. (1981) *Job Creation and the Council: Local Government and the Struggle for Full Employment*, Pamphlet No. 78, Institute for Workers' Control.

Welbur, D. (1987) 'Jobs in the inner city', paper given at Institute of Planning Studies, University of Nottingham, May.

Williams, R. (1975) *The Country and the City*, Paladin.

Wolfenden, J. (1978) *The Future of Voluntary Organizations*, Croom Helm.

Young, K., Mason, C. and Mills, E. (1980) *Urban Governments and Economic Change*, SSRC Inner Cities Working Party, 'The Inner City in Context' II, SSRC, London.

Young, K. and Mason, C. (1983) 'The significance of urban economic development programmes', in K. Young and C. Mason (eds) *Urban Economic Development: New Roles and Relationships*, Macmillan.

Young, M. and Wilmott, P. (1957) *Family and Kinship in East London*, Routledge & Kegan Paul.

Index

Area basis for urban policy 19, 55 ff., 73, 138 ff., 143
Area Management Trials 26

Batly, R. 18
Benington, J. 140, 144
Blunkett, D. and Hodge, M. 170
Boddy, M. 99, 110
Brown, M. and Madge, N. 61

Centralization 28
Church of England x
Clarke, Kenneth 30, 105
Committee of Public Accounts 53, 61
Community action 145 ff.
Community Action Programme (USA) 13–14
Community Development Projects 5, 20, 21, 75, 130, 140, 148
Comprehensive Community Programme 25

Dearlove, J. 144
Deindustrialization 92, 109
Department of the Environment 95, 105, 112, 116, 126
    Urban Programme Management Initiative 28, 95, 118
Dunleavy, P. xi, 48

Edelman, M. 43
Edwards, J. 18

Enterprise Zones 52, 92

Financial Institutions Group 28
Fiscal crisis 38, 48
Ford Foundation 9
Friedland, R. 42

Golding, P. 3
Goodwin, M. and Duncan, S. 99, 105
Gough, I. 39

Hall, S. 44
Harrington, M. 6
Heseltine, M. 28, 54, 95
Higgins, J, x
Holterman, S. 61
Home Office 19, 22, 130, 140
    Urban Deprivation Unit 24
Housing Investment Programme 50, 53, 71, 166

Immigration 5, 15, 26
Inner Area Programme
    as poverty programme 33 ff.
    as symbolic 43 ff.
    bidding process 78 ff., 119 ff., 125, 143, 152 ff., 162, 169
    experimentation 84 ff., 91, 113, 165, 167
    partnership 46, 69–70, 77, 85, 130, 133, 137, 143, 147–8, 153, 159 ff., 165
    self-help in 46, 70, 133, 137 ff.

redirection of resources 50, 76, 87, 94, 165, 167
Priority Zones 68, 73 ff.
slippage 81, 119, 124
Inner Area Studies 23, 26, 27, 75, 94

Jenkin, P. 110, 139
Johnson, L. 12, 14, 130

Kennedy, J. F. 10

Lawless, P. 26
Leach, S. and Stewart, J. 71, 80
Leicester
  Inner Area Programme 53, 67 ff., 134, 150 ff., 169
  poverty in 165
  race issue in 26
  Task Force 31
Leicester City Council 75, 77, 81, 89, 91, 113, 115, 144, 145, 158
Leicester Mercury 31
Local economic development 91, 96 ff., 113
Local Government Act (1972), Section 137 89, 95, 97, 119, 168

McConahay, J. B. 12
Mackintosh, M. and Wainwright, H. 110
Manpower Services Commission 97 ff., 127
Marshall, M. and Mawson, I. 96
Middleton, S. 3
Mollenkopf, J. H. 12, 13
Moynihan, D. 6, 7, 130, 147
Municipal socialism 91, 106, 167, 168

O'Connor, J. 39
Oppenheim, C. 168

Patten, J. 170

Piven, F. and Cloward, R. 7, 11, 14
Police 54, 164
Policy for the Inner Cities (1977 White Paper) x, 27
Policy Planning Systems 71, 80, 83
Poverty 16, 23, 45, 56, 74, 128, 131, 137, 145, 166
Poverty Programmes 33 ff., 36, 49, 71, 130, 132, 137, 140, 146, 148, 163, 165
  in United States 3–15
Powell, Enoch 15, 18, 133
Privatization 28
Public expenditure 39, 51, 86
Public participation in urban policy, 130 ff., 145, 148, 163, 167

Race dimension to urban programmes 5–7, 15–16, 17, 27, 169
Rate capping 83, 92, 149
Rate Support Grant 50, 53
Ridley, N. 170
Riots and urban violence
  in UK x, 15, 17–18, 28, 44, 46, 53, 95, 115, 169
  in USA 11

Saunders, P. xi
Scarman Report 54
Sears, D. 12
Shore, P. x, 25, 26, 43, 165
Stedman Jones, G. 3

Task Force 30, 92
  in Leicester 31
Tebbit, N. ix
Thatcher, Mrs M. ix, 21
  urban policy under 28
Townsend, P. 16, 59
Trippier, D. 167

Unemployment x

Urban Development Corporations 28, 92
Urban Development Grants 51

Voluntary sector 67, 78, 84, 104, 119, 125, 128, 133, 140 ff., 148, 150, 157, 161, 169

Walker, P. x, 23
Ward, M. 107
Watts district of Los Angeles 11
Wilson, Harold 18, 133
Wolfenden Committee 141

Young, Lord David 30, 167